GIFTED CHILDREN
and the
Brentwood Experiment

GIFTED CHILDREN
and the
Brentwood Experiment

Edited by S. A. BRIDGES, M.A., B.Sc., Ph.D.

London
Sir Isaac Pitman & Sons Ltd.

First published 1969

SIR ISAAC PITMAN AND SONS LTD.
Pitman House, Parker Street, Kingsway, London, W.C.2
P.O. Box 6038, Portal Street, Nairobi, Kenya

SIR ISAAC PITMAN (AUST.) PTY. LTD.
Pitman House, Bouverie Street, Carlton, Victoria 3053, Australia

PITMAN PUBLISHING CORPORATION (S.A.) PTY. LTD.
P.O. Box 7721, Johannesburg, Transvaal, S. Africa

PITMAN PUBLISHING CORPORATION
20 East 46th Street, New York, N.Y. 10017

SIR ISAAC PITMAN (CANADA) LTD.
Pitman House, 381–383 Church Street, Toronto, 3

THE COPP CLARK PUBLISHING COMPANY
517 Wellington Street, Toronto, 2B

MADE IN GREAT BRITAIN AT THE PITMAN PRESS, BATH
F9—(G.4613)

Preface

AT the present time there is an increasing interest in the problems of the education of gifted children, marked by the beginning of research in these problems and by the foundation of the National Association for Gifted Children. This interest appears throughout the history of education but it has tended to wax and wane. The present increase in interest is dictated partly by economic considerations, partly by international rivalries on earth and in space, and partly as a reaction to certain sociological trends in education which seem to many people to be leading to a lowering of standards. The movement towards making provision for children who seem to be more gifted than others, whatsoever the reason for or origin of giftedness, rouses suspicion in many minds that we are heading for a new stratification of society with a kind of dictatorship, sometimes referred to as a meritocracy. The real justification, however, for considering the education of gifted children is the same as that for handicapped children, namely, an attempt to fulfil the provision, under the 1944 Act, of education for all children according to their age, aptitude and ability.

The Plowden Report makes two contributions to the approach to dealing with the problems of the education of gifted children. Firstly, by laying stress on the importance of the developmental age the Report makes possible a breakaway, at least in ideas, from the all too rigid adherence to the chronological age, which is one factor only in dealing with the development of children and their readiness for more advanced work, as, for example, in the field of abstraction. Piaget's work becomes much more valuable when the developmental age is preferred to the chronological. The second contribution is contained in Chapter 22 of the Report which deals specifically with the education of gifted children. There is a cautious admission that there may be special needs and reference is made to the work carried on at Brentwood. The final conclusion is that further research is required into this whole field.

No studies comparable to those of Terman [48]† in the U.S.A. have been carried out in this country but there have been people who have been interested in gifted children. Amongst others are Sir Cyril Burt [9 and 10], Mary Waddington [52] and Dr. W. D. Wall [53a and 53b], and at present there are several workers in the field. J. B. Shields has studied fifty gifted children and has confirmed some of the findings of Terman with regard to their superior mental, physical and character qualities. Professor Tempest is studying a group of gifted children who are being taught as a class for four years in a junior school. Liam Hudson [29] has studied gifted boys from the point of view of convergent and divergent thinkers and has published his findings in a book called *Contrary Imaginations*. The National Bureau for Co-operation in Child Care, under Dr. Kellmer-Pringle, is studying a number of gifted children from the large cohort of children which has been studied from birth in 1958. Mr. Meyer at Millfield School has catered for a large number of gifted children, and has taken a special interest in those gifted children who, for one reason or another, have not been deriving the benefit they should from the schools that they have attended previously. Colleges of Education are bringing the problem to the notice of their students, many of whom seek help from Brentwood or from Mr. Robb, Psychologist to the Essex County Education Committee, who has done much to stimulate the interest now shown widely.

Attempts to deal with the education of gifted children have taken a variety of forms. The commonest of these in this country have been in the form of selective education or else homogeneous groupings, otherwise known as streaming. Some people have advocated the establishment of special schools for the educationally super-normal as well as for the sub-normal, but this proposal has not received much support in this country. There is little evidence to justify the proposal, and in any case, it is contrary to the prevailing ideas based on a sociological approach to education. There seems to be a stronger case for homogeneous grouping, but, if this is to be persisted with, it must not be based on crude measurements of one factor. The gradual acceptance of the developmental age and of

† Numbers in square brackets refer to publications listed in the bibliography (page 155).

the idea of sets which are not based on chronological age may lead to more adequate provision for all children, including the gifted. Even in selective education, there is evidence that the level of aspiration for the gifted pupils is often too low so that there is inadequate stimulation or incentive to attempt to realize their full potential.

Another method is that of acceleration, which tends to over-ride the rigidity of classes based on chronological age. Acceleration has often been helpful to gifted children but it has certain limitations. The first of these is that the acceleration may have to be so great as to lead to other problems. A pre-pubertal girl of 11 in a fourth-year grammar-school class of young post-pubertal women is an extreme case but it serves to illustrate the kind of difficulty that can arise. A second limitation arises where work in a subject is progressive so that the present work depends on what has been done in the past. Acceleration, unless a special effort is made to cover the part of the work inevitably missed, may lead to a temporary backwardness, which is likely to have a bad effect especially in younger children. Acceleration, therefore, is not a solution in all cases.

Another of the common educational terms is "enrichment," which is made to stand for so many different ideas that it really defies simple definition. For some teachers it tends to mean occupying the brighter and faster workers with more difficult examples, but this is of doubtful educational value where the children have already mastered the underlying principles. For others it means sending the brighter children off to the library or outside the school to carry on personal studies: such work may be guided by the teacher or the children may be left to work entirely by themselves. In some schools enrichment takes place in the form of clubs, sometimes during regular school hours, sometimes outside school hours. An outstanding example of this is in Semerhoff's work at Sevenoaks. Week-end classes or Saturday morning groups are held in some cases. Another form is that of the summer camp, popular in parts of the U.S.A., and now being developed by the National Association for Gifted Children in this country. In these camps there are studies, and persons of eminence in arts and science may be invited to take part. The work at Brentwood can probably be placed under this heading.

The purpose of the present book is threefold. The first purpose is to review the work that has been done and is being done at Brentwood College of Education. We describe this work as experimental, and have not called it research because we have not worked statistically and it has not been possible for us to work with control groups. These limitations have been dictated to a great extent by circumstances. College staff, who participate, and the children, are available for only one afternoon a week for some thirty weeks in the year. For the children this is a very small proportion of the school year and so it is doubtful whether work with so-called controls would be valid. Staff, too, have many commitments, and have voluntarily undertaken to add this weekly commitment to the others. However, despite these limitations, the work has had a considerable effect on other people who are interested in the problems of the education of gifted children, and members of staff have been invited to describe the work done in many other areas. The work has also proved stimulating to the members of staff themselves.

The second purpose is to put on record the lessons that we have learned in the course of the work. These lessons, which are dealt with in the chapters which follow, are important for all children. Certainly most of the participant members of staff and several of the students who have been involved have had to think again about many of the ideas they had previously accepted. It is our hope that readers of this book will find that they too must re-examine some of the ideas on which they have been basing their teaching.

The third purpose of the book is to try to give some help to those teachers who are aware of the presence in their classes of children who are gifted in some way and who are aware also that they are not giving these children the help that they require. In some cases the difficulty arises from sheer numbers—most of the children in our groups come from urban schools in which the classes number 40 to 50 pupils. In other cases the difficulty arises from the special needs of the children themselves. A number of such special needs will be dealt with below. There seems to be a strong case for some sort of advisory service for teachers to help in the handling of such cases. At Brentwood we have had hopes of establishing such an advisory service, but the continual expansion of the College itself has rendered this, so far, an impossibility.

One lesson that we have learned is that there is no simple problem to be solved here. There is, rather, a complex of problems, and so a considerable number of approaches is called for. No single person has the knowledge or experience to deal with these problems and so at Brentwood we have been obliged to build up a staff-team which represents a cross-section of the staff. Each member of the team has made a contribution of some kind to the work as a whole, and for this reason, as well as because of the complexity of the subject, this book is in the form of a symposium.

We wish to thank for their co-operation—

The Essex Education Committee, the Chief Education Officer and Mr. G. C. Robb, M.A., Psychologist to the Committee.

The Divisional Education Officers of Mid-Essex and S. E. Essex.

The Havering Education Committee, Mr. R. C. Betts, B.A., Chief Inspector, and Mrs. I. A. Poulton, B.A., Psychologist to the Committee.

Dr. D. W. Shave, M.Sc., Ph.D., Principal of Brentwood College of Education, and the Heads of Departments.

The Heads of the Schools (Messrs. D. G. F. Davies, J. Davis, J. W. Dodd, C. Ford, J. E. Franklin, A. Gaunt, F. G. Lacey, H. T. Mirrington, A. Smith and Miss M. W. Warren) and Mrs. Jarvis.

Mrs. M. Nunns who typed and improved the script.

S. A. BRIDGES

Contents

        including Gifted Children   *George Miniken*   136

14   Conclusion   *Dr. S. A. Bridges*   153

        Bibliography   155

        Index   159

This book is dedicated to
the memory of Steve Keirl,
an early and valuable
member of our team

1 *The Pilot Scheme*

S. A. BRIDGES, M.A., B.Sc., Ph.D.

DURING the final teaching practice in 1964, members of the Education Department of the College acted as moderators of marks, and so each was able to see a cross-section of the teaching of the student body. One criticism which was made by these tutors was that in many cases the pace of work of the students and of the work set by students was rather slow. For the quicker children the pace was much too slow, so that some children were being held back or else were suffering from boredom. The tutors felt then that they were faced with the problem of making the students aware of the importance of pace of lessons, especially for those children whose attainments and whose ability in class were well above the average. In an attempt to solve this problem, the then Principal Lecturer in Education, Miss M. Pixell, suggested that, as many of the brighter children had already been chosen for selective education, such children might be made available in the College without too many difficulties. This suggestion was put to the Education Authority and approved, and subsequently Head-teachers of certain Junior Schools were approached and invited to co-operate.

What followed was dictated largely by the need to form the group of children as quickly as possible. When the question of criteria arose, it was decided to ask the Heads of some schools, where we already knew that there were some very bright children, to nominate children who had scored highly in the reasoning test used for secondary-school selection. The ceiling of this test was a score of 140 and we received a list of names of all those children whose scores exceeded 130. As a result, we were provided with a list of some twenty children (12 boys and 8 girls) who had already made certain of going to a Grammar School. Some five or six of these children had scored 140, so that the test did not really go high

I

enough to test the pupils adequately. The group seemed to be quite a promising one for our purpose of making at least some of our students realize the needs of such children.

At first these children tended to be referred to as the "bright children," but gradually they began to be called "gifted children." This change in nomenclature may be justified, but it should be made clear that at the time we were not interested so much in the children as in their possible effect on the students. It should also be made clear that neither then nor since have we equated gifted children with high-I.Q. children or children of high reasoning ability. We have kept in mind and have tried to convince our students, and also some of our later groups of children chosen on a criterion of a high-I.Q. score, that giftedness can and does take many forms and that our chief reason for limiting our experimental work to two criteria, high-I.Q. and creativity, has been our very limited resources of staff and time.

Having recruited the children, we then had two questions to answer. The first of these was whether College staff or students should be responsible for teaching the children. As the purpose of the group was to help our students, it was finally decided that the work should be undertaken by students. Volunteers were called for and a number of students in different subjects offered their services. Some students, who had been expected to assist, did not offer themselves and, on inquiry, they explained their unwillingness on the grounds that they felt that they lacked the quickness of mind necessary to deal with quick-witted children. Some of the students had witnessed the testing on Closed Circuit Television of a bright boy (I.Q. 160 on the 1960 revision of the Terman-Merrill Intelligence test) and had been astounded and alarmed by the speed with which the boy had answered the questions put to him by the examining psychologist. It was pointed out to these rather fearful students that there was a good chance that one or two such bright children would appear in their classes and that it would be impossible to avoid the problems raised by this occurrence.

The students who did volunteer may have had doubts about their ability, but they were probably relieved to learn that no group was likely to exceed three or four children. Moreover, in each case they would be working in their own main subject so that their knowledge was likely to be adequate for most occasions and for most of the questions likely to be raised by the children. In fact, all the students concerned soon became interested in the children and their capabilities, and then any lingering doubts disappeared.

As we were to have the children one afternoon a week for some two hours, we had to decide whether the children should have one or two activities in the course of the afternoon. As we were uncertain, we decided that there should be one activity and that within the limits imposed by the number of departments co-operating the children should have a free choice of the field of activity. The ultimate choice was from Nature Study, Physics, Chemistry, Mathematics and Art and Craft. Two or three children chose Nature Study, four or five Physics or Chemistry, eight chose Mathematics, and the rest Art and Craft. Motives underlying the actual choices seemed to be three: a desire to follow up a subject not provided for in school, a desire to make full use of the facilities offered by the College, and a desire to begin work which might help the children in their future studies in the Secondary School. At least two girls chose Mathematics because this was a relatively weak subject and they hoped that they would have some help. At this stage, we were not particularly concerned whether the work might anticipate that likely to be undertaken in the Secondary School. In all our subsequent experiments we have done our utmost to avoid any such anticipation.

At this stage of our work we had given little of our attention to creativity, but we did hope that our students, with only very small groups to deal with, might at least show a creative or imaginative approach to their work. We soon realized that this was too optimistic for a variety of reasons. The first of these was that the students were not sufficiently masters of the teaching of their subject to be capable of departing from more orthodox approaches. Secondly, there was no real demand for anything else from the children, who were satisfied with the excitement of the journey to College and of the splendid facilities made available to them. For the children taking Science there was the fascination of working in laboratories with ample equipment, which they were allowed to use by themselves. For those taking Mathematics there were chances of working with and operating machines which were new to them. For those taking Art and Craft there was again an abundance of equipment together with the freedom to use it. For all the children there was nearly personal attention from an adult, in marked contrast to the crowded classrooms from which they came. Moreover, the schools supplying the children were efficient, but rather formal, and so the children were content with what was in most cases a formal approach of the kind to which they were accustomed.

In providing these excellent facilities we made the assumption that the children would enjoy themselves and wish to come regularly, that they would make full use of their opportunities to work at a high level in any subject field that they had chosen, that they would be capable of a high degree of abstraction, and that the students would benefit greatly from the experience of working with and stimulating these children. In the outcome these assumptions were justified only in part and so we began to learn the lessons which would be useful in the planning of any further work. Let us now look at what actually happened and what we learned.

Our first assumption, that the children would enjoy themselves, was justified and all the children were keen to come again, not just because they were able to escape from the school for an afternoon. Moreover they quickly struck up a good but rather formal relationship with the students taking them. The latter learned to plan enough work to occupy their groups for a period of almost two hours, but generally speaking the periods were too long for the children and students alike and so we decided that in any future work we would divide the afternoon into two roughly equal parts. The students found the work rather exacting, as they were working with two or three children each and this number proved too small in relation to the length of time. So for the sake of the students as well as for the children we decided that in future we should have somewhat larger groups.

Our assumption that the students would benefit was justified, but we had evidence that without careful guidance from staff the benefit was rather limited. On the whole the students who had volunteered for this work were conscientious rather than imaginative or adventurous, so that the work chosen in Science, Mathematics and Nature Study tended to be akin to much of the work set in a first year of a Secondary School where restrictions are imposed by the numbers of children who have to be crowded into a laboratory or classroom. In the field of methods the approach was not very stimulating or imaginative and on occasion a student would treat a group of three as if they were a class of thirty or more. This seemed to arise in part from a detached attitude on the part of some of the children, to which further reference will be made below. It became clear that in any future work College staff would have to play a bigger part and that as far as possible staff should have some say in the choice of students. Much more guidance would be required and probably some sort of team work between staff and students would be necessary following the launching of new groups, preferably by skilled members of the College staff.

At this early stage in our work we were not sure what we could expect or were expecting from these children. We were aware that they performed satisfactorily in school at a level sufficient to lead them on to selective education, but we were aware also that for one reason or another they did not always work up to what we thought their potential might be. We knew that most children who scored as well as they had done in the selection tests tended to be regarded by their teachers as successful pupils, and that most parents were satisfied if their children "passed the 11+." We knew also that the children came from schools with large classes in which much of the kind of work which we could offer was out of the question. As we thought about the children and their possible performance we came to expect a sudden burgeoning of ability and effort which would accord with the high scores on the reasoning tests. As it turned out, all the children performed reasonably well; nevertheless we were left with a feeling of disappointment. When we looked further into the matter we perceived at least two possible causes of this feeling.

One of the causes lay in the attitude of the children which seemed to lessen the effect of the challenge which the students were trying to make. The children had long since become accustomed to a certain level of expectation on the part of their teachers and also probably of their parents. The result was that on the whole their level of aspiration or demand upon themselves was relatively low. For years they had mostly been coasting because they had found it easy with a certain amount of effort to maintain a good position in class, and since this position proved satisfactory to both school and home they were satisfied. When we became aware of this attitude to school work (it did not seem to apply to some of their outside activities) we did our utmost to try to alter it, but the three or four months we had at our disposal proved much too short to make much impression. Once again we realized that we were up against a problem which we would require time and skill to solve. One way in which we might tackle the time problem was to choose children from a lower age group who might be less set in their ways: hence our later recruitments, mainly at the age of eight. The required skill would have to come from the College staff.

The other cause lay in the methods of working and a certain tendency to impatience. For example, in some of the Science experiments, one or two of the children seemed to anticipate the result towards which the student wished them to work. Whenever this happened, the children seemed to find the actual winding up of the experiment tedious. It was as if they felt that they had learned all they were likely to, and so they would have preferred to abandon the rest of the experiment and proceed to the next. It has been suggested that this is a manifestation of what is sometimes called the "butterfly" mind, which tires quickly of each succeeding interest and so hops on to another, leading to a wide but superficial knowledge. This might be the explanation where there are many novel alternatives together, as in the Science Museum; but this tendency continued to show itself even after the first novelty had worn off. Whatever the explanation, we decided that in future work we should try to stress the necessity for patient and accurate work if we wished to obtain really worthwhile results.

2 *The First Two Groups*

S. A. BRIDGES, M.A., B.Sc., Ph.D.

LARGELY as a result of the lessons we had learned from our work with the Pilot Group, we decided that in recruiting new groups we must select younger children, so that we should be able to study them for a much longer period, and so that we might begin work with them before they had grown used to taking school life very easily. In consequence, we determined to recruit two groups, one of nine-year-olds and the other of eight-year-olds, so that we should be able to work with them for periods of two and three years respectively. As we would have the youngsters for only one afternoon a week for about 30 weeks each year, it was obvious that the longer period was likely to prove the more useful to us.

The next problem was that of the criterion by which the children should be chosen. Help was sought from the psychologist to the Essex Education Committee, and he suggested that we should use the 1960 revision of the Terman-Merrill Intelligence Test, which has a ceiling of 170. As he was willing to organize the testing, we accepted this suggestion and proposed certain schools in which the testing might be carried out. Some of the schools selected had already been represented in our Pilot Group. The children tested were nominated by head-teachers in consultation with class-teachers. It is possible, as a result, that some children of high potential were missed, but the psychologist found a considerable number of children of I.Q.s of 140 and over. We decided that this would be our minimum, but three children with scores in the 130s were accepted because the psychologists conducting the tests made special recommendations. Several of the 38 children whom we ultimately invited to the College had scores of 160 or over: five were marked at 170+. Eleven of the 38 children came from one class; in another case, five children of I.Q.s of 160 or over came from the same class. Although an average does not mean very much in such cases, it may be of interest to note that it was over 155. There were 24 boys and 14 girls: in all our groups chosen on I.Q. scores, boys have been in the majority; in our creativity groups, girls have been in the majority.

When the groups were finally formed, it was found that there were 17 children in the nine-year-old group and 21 in the younger, this latter group including the 11 children from one class. Some information was then sought from the schools about the homes of the children and generally speaking we found that the children came mainly from homes of fairly high socio-economic status, the parents in a few cases being graduates. We had noticed this in our Pilot Group, and in choosing our schools for the new experiment we deliberately included two from which we hoped to recruit one or two children from less economically favoured homes. We were not really successful, as even from these homes the children had a favourable home background, which was reflected in their vocabulary and in their attitudes. This result was, of course, not unexpected, but we still hope that in some of our future work we shall be able to find and study children from homes where the status and the encouragement of the parents are of less significance, in a favourable sense, than that of the majority of our children. There were, however, one or two problems connected with homes, and one of these will be referred to below. One thing is certain, as far as the parents were concerned: all were most pleased that their children had been chosen for this experimental work.

Because it had been impressed upon us, from a number of different sources, that the child of high ability and advanced vocabulary tends to be isolated from his classmates, we decided to investigate the sociometric status of the children in relation to their classmates. For this reason, after we had decided on the classes from which the children would be chosen but before the psychologists had begun testing, we used one of Moreno's techniques. Each child was asked to write down in order the four children he would like to work with in a group. Sociograms were drawn up and when the children were eventually chosen their status was studied. In the majority of cases it was found that the children concerned were moderately popular. In only two cases out of the 38 were the children the most popular, one girl (I.Q. 140) having 21 choices, including several from boys. A few were near-isolates, one boy having only one choice. When the test was repeated a year later, to try to discover whether the specialized treatment of these children throughout the year had affected their position, it was found that there were few changes of significance. One boy who had had seven choices now had none— he was a spoiled child and might have been better left out of our scheme. The most noticeable changes were in the reverse direction, the near-isolates having improved their status. The schools reported that the children not chosen had shown little resentment against those who had been: the sociometric test seemed to substantiate this.

The schools from which the children came tended on the whole to be formal with an insistence on school uniform, so that most of the boys were dressed in blazers and shorts and the girls, too, mostly wore blazers and school frocks. The schools laid a good deal of stress on order and discipline and so we wondered what our approach should be. Generally speaking, the College relationships are very informal, and so both staff and students tended to be informal with the children. Most of these accepted the freedom from formality as if they had always been accustomed to it. Several of the children were clearly very advanced socially, and these boys and girls, the latter being the more socially developed on the whole, set an example which was followed by all except one or two of the children, who might be described as problem children. One such boy, who had been specially recommended by one of the psychologists, found it difficult to fit in, preferring at times in the afternoon break to run about shrieking his head off, but, although he never quite settled down like some of the mature girls, he was largely a normal citizen by the time he left, three years later, for the Secondary School.

The commonest problems of the children were boredom unless highly stimulated and the tendency to take things too easily, but these problems will be dealt with specifically in the next chapter. There were other problems, however, of which some examples follow.

The sociometric test had shown that there were some near-isolates and so we tried to find out the probable causes of this isolation. In one or two cases the children seemed to be shy, but the isolation was of a normal type and not linked with giftedness. In two or three cases the isolation tended to be connected with giftedness. For example, a bright, well-developed girl, who had an uncharacteristic passion for serious drama, found that her coevals of 8+ years had no wish to discuss such matters with her: indeed they were rather impatient with her and would sometimes not speak with her at all. Another child found the making of contacts difficult because he was so uncertain of himself, consequent on his difficulties at home. The son of relatively elderly parents, who were a generation and a half ahead of him, he could find little understanding of his problems at home and he seemed to feel that nobody else could. He was very bright and thoughtful with introverted tendencies. He was one of those who made most progress during the first year, and when the sociometric test was repeated after a year instead of one choice he was chosen four times, and three of these choices were mutual.

Another boy, whose I.Q. was 170, and who was quite popular in his class, was sometimes a nuisance to his teacher and occasionally was a little obstreperous at the College. On investigation, it became clear that the parents were not nearly as bright as their child, so that they found it very difficult to understand what he was talking about and at times his speed of thought, especially in the form of retorts, bewildered and annoyed them. They recognized the fact that they had a bright child, but instead of being pleased they were upset. Their lack of understanding often puzzled the boy and when this occurred he reacted unfavourably in school. In still another case there was evidence that the parents were not only less bright than their boy but also rather jealous of his powers and achievements. More serious perhaps still was the case of the boy with an I.Q. of 170+ with a very favourable home who was less fortunate in his teacher. The latter seemed to resent the ability of the boy and the fact that he had been chosen for our group. The situation was not eased by the boy's possession of an effervescent sense of humour, whereas his teacher seemed devoid of this quality. Whenever an opportunity occurred (as it inevitably did from time to time, because of his sense of humour) the teacher dressed the boy down so that he dissolved in tears and became nervous and all too easily upset. His behaviour at the College was exemplary and he flourished there.

His experience at the College, together with the eventual departure of the teacher to another district, helped him considerably, and, although remaining rather sensitive, he went forward to the Secondary School with confidence.

The attainments of the children were normally satisfactory and in those cases where class positions were available these children usually occupied the top places: there were exceptions to which reference will be made below. Whether the high class positions are adequate proof that the children are realizing most of their potential will be discussed in the next chapter. Needless to say, their greatest achievement tended to be in the field of vocabulary and reading. In several cases standardized reading tests had been applied in the schools, and wherever this had been done the children seemed well above the average. Several of the nine-year-olds and some of the eight-year-olds had reading ages 5 to 6 years above their chronological age; indeed for several the reading scales had too low a ceiling to spread them out. These results corresponded to the results of the Terman-Merrill scores on the verbal parts of the test—some of the children had been able to deal with the problems on the Superior Adult tests. All the children were members of libraries, either in school or in the locality. Several had personal libraries which contained books on science as well as story-books, and some boys read regularly "Understanding Science."

There were two differences which were quite clearly marked. The first of these was in the speed of working as shown in the approach to the tests set at the College. For example, in one or two of the reading and vocabulary tests, where there was a time-limit, some of the children did not complete the tests, and yet that part which they had completed might be near perfect. There were, of course, those who worked very fast indeed, sometimes in a slapdash way, and who managed to complete a test but making errors which they could have corrected if they had taken the trouble to read over the test again within the time which they had to spare. Some showed the same impatience which we had already noted in the Pilot Group; others, again, seemed to have become so accustomed to a leisurely pace of work that they found it difficult to work at the speed required by the time-limit. A natural question was whether this relative slowness (their pace was probably still somewhat above average for children as a whole) was temperamental or whether it was largely the product of conditioning in the school, where there was no pressure to increase the speed of reading or of working. A similar variation in pace was noticeable in oral work. Some children were obviously accustomed to put up their hands in a leisurely manner to answer questions; their leisureliness in the ordinary classroom did not prevent their being amongst the first to offer an answer. This tended to apply mostly to boys and girls who came from classes where there were no other, or else only one or two other children of the same ability. Where there were several children of high ability, there was clearly a tendency for the children to raise their hands quickly when a question was asked. When the children who responded in a leisurely fashion found themselves in a group of their intellectual peers, they soon found that they were left behind as others quickly answered. Two or three of the children passed through an unhappy period, but gradually there was a general smartening-up until the pace of the response of the group was almost uniform.

The second difference was in the field of Mathematics. For most of the children, Mathematics still meant Arithmetic, despite the fact that the schools mostly included other aspects of Mathematics. When a Mathematical Insight Test was applied, the results showed a wide range of results, although only two children, a boy and a girl, did rather badly. As there was a time-limit, some youngsters suffered from their being accustomed to working at a moderate pace, as in the cases described in the preceding paragraph. What they did they did well, but their scores, in relation to the total number of items, was disappointing. Yet a few weeks later several of these disappointing youngsters were to trouble the students responsible for the groups of children who chose Mathematics, which included Set Theory, with the speed of their understanding and the perspicacity of their questions. The students on several occasions had to take defensive measures by promising that they would find out the answers to questions before the next meeting. One of the most persistent askers of these perplexing questions was the girl who had done so poorly on the Mathematical Insight Test: indeed, during the test she had dissolved into tears. Her trouble seems to have been a phobia for Arithmetic; once she was free from the fears that calculation seemed to bring, she developed rapidly. By the time she left us for the Secondary School, the phobia seemed to have disappeared. The boy who did badly, on the other hand, suffered from some blockage, which meant that in Arithmetic he worked slowly but on the whole accurately. The application of diagnostic tests revealed that there was no fundamental weakness. The boy, who was the youngest in the Senior Group and who was in that group because of his class, whereas by age he should have been in the Junior Group, was well aware of his trouble, which he had diagnosed. Despite his awareness and despite our efforts to help him, he made no great improvement, but his slowness did not seem to affect him to any extent in dealing with ideas of Implication or Inference in Mathematical Logic.

Once we had chosen our groups of children, we were faced with the problem of what kind of programme to provide them with, and here there were three considerations. We had to remember that the experiment had begun as an effort to help our students to become aware of the existence of bright children and their special needs in the classroom. The question then arose as to how the students were to be recruited. Fortunately, several of the students who had participated in the Pilot Group were still available and most willing to carry on, all the more so as they had chosen "The Education of Bright Children" as their personal study. Other students were recruited partly as the result of their choice of a personal study and partly by nomination of the Departments which had offered or been invited to take part in the new experiment. Normally, students were allowed to offer their main subject, as it was felt that in teaching such boys and girls they required the help that a mastery of their main subject would afford. This consideration for the students meant a limitation in the number of activities which could be provided for the children. On the whole, the students who made up the teams were above average both in their main study and in their practical teaching. As the students had to be recruited from the three-year course, for time-table reasons, they tended to come from our younger students, who had themselves left school within the previous five years or so.

From the point of view of the benefit of the children, the chief consideration was that they should enjoy the experience to such an extent that they would look forward eagerly to each Friday afternoon. Naturally enough there was an initial pleasure in having an afternoon away from school, travelling some miles by coach or van, and having the rich facilities provided by the College. Novelty can, however, wear off, and if the children were to begin balancing what they were missing on a Friday afternoon, perhaps games or swimming, then they were not enjoying themselves sufficiently. The pleasure must continue, and this could be done only by ensuring that the work each week was interesting and challenging. To be challenging for such children, the work must be more advanced than they were accustomed to in school, and yet it must not merely be an anticipation of what they would do later in school life, since that would be to ensure boredom later on, thus undoing any good that we might do. Nor must it be merely harder work of the kind they were already doing, since that would soon lead to boredom in the present. Again, the programmes must be suited to the age and development of the children, and so we decided that we should have different programmes for the senior and the junior groups. The question of a measure of choice arose, but it was decided that this was not important at the beginning of the experiment: it would become more important and more practicable when we had come to know the children and when they had come to know more about us and more about their own preferences.

The third consideration was the need for a balance in the activities offered. We found that on the whole the boys had a bias towards Science and Mathematics, and, although several of them enjoyed Literature and Art and Craft, they tended to regard these as not too important compared with Mathematics. Even amongst the girls there was a bias towards Mathematics, but this seemed to be largely the result of parental prompting. It is, perhaps, significant that in the four years of our experimental work only one girl has chosen Science where a free choice was offered. On the other hand, where girls have had to study Science, willy-nilly, they seem to have derived as much pleasure from it as the boys. To ensure this balance which we considered essential, we have included some form of the Arts in all our schemes: it has taken the forms, at different times, of Drama, Closed Circuit Television Drama, Art and Craft,

Needlecraft, and Music. This balance will be observed in both the programmes outlined below.

In the case of the Senior Group, it was decided that in the course of each afternoon there would be two activities, the first concerned with language, which would be in the hands of two senior members of staff, and Mathematics, which would be taken by students. Language was a very wide term and the programme varied considerably. When the group was taken by the Head of the English Department, who was very interested in the project, the activities included discussion, drama, some technical work on English and work involving tape-recordings. On one occasion the children were fascinated by a recording of extracts from Chaucer which led to a discussion and some further study of the development of English language. For work as challenging as this, it soon became obvious that a wide knowledge of the language and a high degree of teaching skill were necessary to stimulate and then to satisfy the curiosity of these intelligent children.

The alternative programme consisted sometimes of discussion, sometimes of written work, sometimes of the application of tests. For example, discussions took place on such topics as "Why did Socrates refuse to accept the offer of his friends to help him to escape from prison?" or the versatility of a man like Leonardo da Vinci, or the life and ideas of a man like Einstein. These may seem too abstruse for children of nine years, but in this field these were no ordinary children, and the present writer, who was responsible for this part of the programme, was constantly amazed by the high quality of the discussions and of the answers given by the children to his own questions, and also by the fascinating variety of the questions they asked. Not all the children took a great part in some of these discussions, but even the quieter ones were capable of a sudden flash of inspiration. The most surprising feature of this aspect of the work was less the breadth of the knowledge of the children, considerable as that was, than the breadth of their thinking. It was clear that they had thoughts and thought links that were quite unsuspected by the adult world. On the other hand, when it came to written work, there was little evidence of the same quality of thought. This was an experience shared by the Head of the English Department. This will be discussed further in the next chapter:

suffice it at present to say that on the whole the written work, although satisfactory technically and although likely to pass muster in the classroom, was almost always disappointing. The tendency was for the work to be churned out with the least possible manifestation of interest or of response to a challenge.

To try to overcome this, attempts were made to use pictures taken from some of the well-known projective tests. Although these are usually intended for individual application and an oral response, with these children carefully selected pictures were given to individual children and they were invited to tell the story as suggested by the picture. Once again, the results were disappointing, but this was not felt to be the inevitable outcome of a foolish procedure. As will be suggested below, it seems more likely that it was the result of a long-term conditioning, since the work which we considered disappointing must often have been accepted as satisfactory in class: this is not surprising when we reflect on the very large classes from which our children came. In a very few cases children were stimulated by the projective pictures to respond in the way expected by the psychologists who had devised the tests. In these cases the stories were of no great literary worth, but they did help us towards a greater understanding of the young authors.

Some of the children seemed happier in another field, that of simple basic Logic. They quickly picked up the concepts of premises, syllogisms, undistributed middles and what constitutes fallacious reasoning. While some of the boys and girls showed that they felt that they were being challenged, others did not respond readily to this type of stimulus. On the other hand, when problems of inductive and deductive reasoning, of the type to be found in Valentine's Higher Reasoning Tests, were presented, there was a better response. One of the lessons which we were trying to teach was that in the attempt to solve a problem one might find that there was insufficient data to arrive at a definite conclusion, while on other occasions there might well be irrelevant data which had first to be identified and then eliminated before a solution became possible. This lesson seemed to be learned by most of the children, but there were two difficulties which had first to be overcome. The first of these was the prolonged conditioning of their schooling, so that they expected a neat, satisfying answer to every problem set: in Arithmetic there was one answer to most of the problems, which could be ticked off as correct. This conditioning may be less effective in the schools as a more open-ended approach is made to school-work. The second difficulty was linked with the first, and showed itself in a feeling of dissatisfaction and almost of annoyance when the problem, although soluble, offered alternative answers. This is not unusual in Mathematics in the Secondary School, but it has not been common in the past in the Primary School. An example occurred with a problem on the lines of Valentine's problems, of which of two men could have committed a murder. The children mostly welcomed such a problem, but, when it became clear that the data were not sufficient to establish which was guilty, some of the children recognized this fact but added some such remark as, "But I think X was the more likely murderer." Only gradually did the majority of the children grow used to the idea that they must be prepared to accept the challenge of such problems, even if there was no certainty that they would be able to reach a definite conclusion.

After a year it became obvious that there would have to be some changes for the second year, especially as the students responsible for the work in Mathematics were leaving. It was equally clear that some of the children were ready for a change also, and so the situation was reviewed. It was decided that as far as possible the language activities would be carried on as before, except that an attempt would be made to bring more students into this work. As the Art and Craft and the Science Departments were willing to co-operate, it was decided that the children should be given a choice of activity for the second part of the afternoon. Three subjects would be available, Mathematics, Science or Art and Craft, and a free choice was allowed. Four children opted to continue with Mathematics (two almost certainly because of parental pressure), six chose Science (five boys and one girl) and the remaining six (one boy left to attend another school) chose Art and Craft. Facilities were greatest for Art and Craft and the activities included pottery as well as painting. The artistic abilities of the children varied considerably: some of the children tended to produce more interesting work than they had done in our language activities. In all the three aspects of the optional work the students were enthusiastic: they had deliberately chosen the topic of the Education of Bright Children as their personal study in Education. In Science, the emphasis was on practical experimental work, and, although there were some signs of the impatience to which reference was made in the previous chapter, this was less in evidence. The influence of the girl, who was very well developed socially and much more mature than any of the boys, seemed to be of importance in containing the effervescent enthusiasm of the boys. The average I.Q. for this group was about 160 and it was noticeable how quickly they mastered the lessons which the students prepared. There seemed to be ample justification for allowing the children to choose at least part of their activities.

This principle of choice was extended to the Junior Group but not in the first year. On arrival, the children were divided up into groups for language activities. An attempt was made to ensure that the groups contained boys and girls from different schools and also one or two of those with the highest I.Q.s. Students, mainly from the English Department, had offered or been nominated to conduct these groups. The students were made aware of the high reading age of the children and urged to challenge them with advanced work. On the whole the activities planned by the students, who could, if they wished, consult members of the College staff, were rather orthodox and not so very different from what some of the children were doing in their schools. There were discussions, some reading of literature, some dramatic work, and a number of attempts at stimulating creative writing. The students ran up against the same difficulties as had been experienced with the Senior Group, but at least the children in the Junior Groups were a year younger and had undergone a year less of schooling. Much good work was done but the children were rarely "stretched" as we had hoped they might be. The reason for this was the inexperience of the students, who were face to face with problems which were rarely included in the books which they had read. We learned one very important lesson here, but we shall discuss this in the next chapter. Suffice it here to say that the students, all of whom realized the difficulty of the job they had undertaken, almost certainly learned more from the work with the children than the latter did from them, and that the first team of students passed on some of the benefit of their experience to those who succeeded them.

Considerable thought was given to the possible activities for the second part of the afternoon. Three College departments had offered to help, Art and Craft, Music, and Physical Education. It was felt that there should be three groups, one a large one of twelve children for Creative Activities in Physical Education, a small one for Music to consist of children specially recommended by their schools as being musically talented, and the third group would go to Art and Craft. It would have been possible to offer the children a choice, but it was felt that this might lead to a group which was too big for the musical facilities available and another too small for the dance activities. In these circumstances it was resolved that the largest group should be picked first and that, in choosing children for this group, use should be made of the results of the sociometric test. This meant placing the children with the fewest choices in this group, along with some of those who had been high up on the scale of popularity. The actual I.Q. variations were ignored. This group would have activities based on working together rather than on individual work, and it was hoped that some of the children with problems would have a chance to work out their problems and to acquire some friends. The activities might not always be a challenge to high intellectual qualities, but they would have some social value, especially, we hoped, for those children who were over-tense and too much pre-occupied with success in the intellectual field. As one student put it, "Crawling round a hall floor on your bare knees reduces all children, however high or low their I.Q., to the same level." As the activities consisted of mime, dance and acting in response to music and other situations, the children were brought together in both dignified and undignified ways. At first, most of the children remained conspicuous individualists who showed a great deal of uncertainty and a clumsiness which was, in part at least, the result of their not being able to let themselves go. Under the stimulation and guidance of highly skilled members of the College staff, and of enthusiastic Physical Education students, the group began to weld together and to treat the activities more seriously. With these developments the children seemed happier and they began to look forward to their programmes. It was clear that some of the more diffident children began to show more confidence in themselves and were better able to establish relationships with other children. Although we realize that other agencies than ourselves were contributing to their social development, there was some evidence that progress was in part due to our experiment.

The Music group were taken by a member of staff who introduced them to Composition, and the three girls concerned seemed to enjoy the work and the inspiration. Unfortunately, after a time the Department became overloaded with duties and so had to withdraw from the experiment. The girls were then asked whether they would like to join the Art and Craft Group, and they agreed that they would. They enjoyed their new activities, which included painting inside and outside the College, various forms of printing, and pottery so much that when later they were given the opportunity to change, they said that they were only too happy to carry on with Art and Craft.

At the end of the first year it was decided that the Dance group had served its purpose and, as other experimental groups were being formed in which the Physical Education Department was being invited to take part, that the children should be given the choice of activities for the following two years. The language activities would be carried on with a fresh team of students who had chosen this kind of work for their personal study. Although the nature of the activities was not greatly changed, the children were ready for a fresh approach, and so the new students were welcomed. Meanwhile, the children in the Dance group were asked whether they would prefer Art and Craft or Science, while those with the Art and Craft group were asked whether they wished to change to Science. In the outcome, most of the boys in the Dance group opted for Science and two or three boys chose to change from Art and Craft. The Science group consisted, therefore, entirely of boys, while the Art and Craft group had a majority of girls. On the whole the choice seems to have been based on a genuine preference and not on any feeling that Science was a more masculine choice than Art and Craft. At the end of the second year the children were again asked whether they would like to change groups for their final year but no child accepted the invitation to change. Moreover, the children remained as eager as ever to come, so that they were obviously satisfied with the respective programmes.

3 Lessons from the First Two Groups

S. A. BRIDGES, M.A., B.Sc., Ph.D.

As a result of our efforts with the pilot scheme and the first two groups, we were at least becoming aware that there were genuine problems connected with the education of children who could score highly in I.Q. tests. It became increasingly clear that those of us who were working with these children had not yet succeeded in realizing the nature of the problems: it became still more abundantly clear that most of the teachers we came into contact with through these children were less aware than we were. To try to help the reader, who may not be convinced that a real problem exists, as there are, after all, those teachers, parents and administrators who assert that bright children can be left to solve any problem by themselves and so need no special help in the educational system—to try to help the reader to realize something of the nature of the problem, I shall now quote from the work of a very bright boy who was rising nine at the time he was writing.

This particular boy, who in appearance was in no way distinguished from the other boys in his class in their blazers and shorts, had an I.Q. in the 160–170 range, and was extremely interested in Science. In his school it was the custom once a week for the children to have a period or lesson-time when they might write a composition or essay in their Topic books. The children were free to choose the Topic. In this boy's book there were several articles on Science interspersed with stories, several of which dealt with secret agents. My quotations come from a Science article and from a story.

(*a*) "Heterocyclic systems. 5-membered rings. Two of the most common five-membered rings are

	The proper rings are	
CH——CH ‖ ‖ CH——CH \ / O	⬠ but they have different formulas	CH——CH ‖ ‖ CH——CH \ / S
Furan		Theophen !

The account continues with a reference to the substitution of an oxygen molecule.

And now, for comparison or contrast, a selection from the composition called "Secret Agents."

(*b*) "*The Man in the Bush*"

"In a lonely but lovely setting a hermit man lived. Nobody ever visited him and nobody ever talked with him. One day a secret agent named Jackson tried to get the hermit to join the county forces, but he resented doing that. Jackson went away and thought about it. He would have to force him! The next evening he went out to find him. He knocked on the door of his hut but no-one replied. He knocked a second and third time and no-one answered. So he searched the surrounding country-side and found, to his annoyance, a notice saying 'Gone to tea!' He went to find the hermit and found him in a café. He was talking to a councillor. So he did belong to a county force."

In most of the work in the Topic book there are few mistakes and there is a quite adult mastery of punctuation, especially of the use of quotation marks in direct speech. The quality varies but the dry humour tends to break out from time to time. Already by nine years this boy had mastered the grammatical aspects of writing, but the material tended towards the orthodox. It may be that the boy should be dismissed as a convergent thinker—a term which will be discussed in the next chapter. It is too easy a way out of the problem. It seems clear that the boy was poised for a considerable advancement in knowledge and in skill, but he was not receiving the help he required for a number of reasons to which further reference will be made below. At the moment it is sufficient if the reader is beginning to see something of the nature of the problems of educating children like this boy.

Another lesson or problem to which our attention was drawn concerned the identification of these children who were gifted in some way and who needed more help than is usually available or is considered necessary. For our groups we had relied on Head-teachers to nominate the children they reckoned as bright, and these children were subsequently tested by psychologists. The majority of the children tested produced good scores, but these did not always reach the figure on which we had arbitrarily decided. Some of the children, who were included on the list of nominations but with some doubts expressed about their potenti-ality, scored highly, and worked well when they came to us. It is possible that we missed some outstanding children, but it is unlikely, as on the whole the Head- and class-teachers showed a fair amount of perception, and in several cases the children were given the benefit of the doubt.

The Head-teachers seemed mainly to use two criteria: one being performance on tests, whether these were standardized or no, and the other being some personal knowledge of the children, together with some knowledge of the home background of the pupils. These would appear to offer a useful basis for identification, but there is always a possibility of a child coming into the category of under-achievers. There are difficulties about the use of this term as writers use it in different ways, while some people claim that there is no meaning in the term. Few teachers would deny, how-ever, that some children do not make full use of their powers in school, and would point to the so-called lazy ones as examples. Our finding has been that under-achievement can occur where a bright child has powers much in excess of what he is called on to use in school: such a child may be first in his class and still, from the viewpoint of his intellectual gifts, be under-achieving. In such cases the measure of under-achievement is obscured by the general satisfaction of a relatively good achievement. Under-achievement, therefore, may go unrecognized, so that a child coasts along quite satisfactorily but with little use of his powers. Standardized tests may help to throw light on this situation, but they may well be inadequate where the child is very bright, and so more adequate tests are required. The I.Q. test does help, but even here there are some children who do not respond and who regard the tests with little enthusiasm, dismissing them as one child did as "parlour tricks."

There are various possible causes of under-achievement, apart from the normal failure to realize that a youngster is so bright that he should be capable of a much higher standard of work than he is turning out regularly. One of these causes is the tendency for teachers to be too easily satisfied with work of a good standard: there is no temptation, especially where the classes are large, for a teacher to ask: "Should this pupil be doing still better?" Parents, too, are often too easily satisfied if the termly report shows that their child is well placed in the class. There are, of course, parents who go to the other extreme, and expect too much, especially from less gifted children. Then, again, children can become too easily satisfied with their work, being pleased and contented if the assessment for the latest piece of work is not less than for the previous. Children, in any case, rarely question the quality of marks, nor do they understand the subjective nature of many of of the assessments made. Although we came across comparatively little evidence in our groups, there are cases where the achievement of children is lower than it could be because children tend to play down their abilities in order to conform with the prevailing standard of the group. A very bright child with a tendency to extraversion does not wish to behave in such a way that he will find himself isolated and so he suppresses any temptation to produce work which will have this effect. One bright boy did hint that he and his classmates who came to us worked often more slowly than they needed to because they did not wish to show how slow the other children were. A far commoner cause, however, was the level of aspiration which for most of the youngsters in our groups was too low. For years they had been accustomed to receive high assessments and praise for work which was considerably above that of the average of the class, and so this was the level at which they had grown accustomed to aim. The success with which children of about average ability have undertaken much of the

Mathematics and Science on Nuffield lines should have convinced us by now that for a long time past we have been under-rating the potentialities of the majority of our school children, and should by now have led us to ask whether our level of aspiration for all children is still too low. Now if this question should be asked generally about our standards in school, then it is still more urgent that we should ask whether our level of aspiration for gifted children is not abysmally, and perhaps disastrously, low. This is the outstanding reason for gifted children not receiving the help which they need, to which they are entitled, and for which they will give a very substantial return.

We soon became acutely aware of some of the manifestations of under-achievement and the low level of aspiration. The most obvious of these was what we in Brentwood have come to call "the stint." Most of our children quickly showed that they had become accustomed to responding to a certain expectation, and they were so used to it that they thought our expectations would be the same. When we asked the children to write, they would ask how many pages, or occasionally lines, we expected, and they were expert at providing the quantity suggested. The quality was treated in much the same way, and some of the children were quite taken aback when we showed dissatisfaction with what they were accustomed to hand in. For example, on one occasion one group was asked to write in 100 words, as interestingly as they could, about themselves. Fairly typical of the responses was the effort which follows, written by a boy of I.Q. 170—

> "I am a boy of almost ten years. I usually wear my school blazer, short, grey corduroy trousers, grey socks and black shoes. I attend . . . Primary School and have reached Class 3. My teacher is a man who may be about 35 years of age. I like the school mostly, but I also like to go home at night when I sometimes watch television and sometimes go to the swimming bath. After another eighteen months I shall be leaving this school and going to a secondary school, but I do not yet know which school it is likely to be."

The young author certainly produced his hundred words, but one feels the effort of it in the details about his clothes and the spinning out of the last sentence. He was eminently satisfied with his work when he handed it in and seemed quite surprised when he was informed that it was rather disappointing, and that, although it conformed to the quantitative condition, it was far from being interesting. In other words, it satisfied the idea of the stint, and there was no call for anything different or better. As was pointed out before, this approach to written work in English persisted for a long time after the children first came to us. The fact that it applied even to the stimulation provided by projective pictures surprised us, and showed us how difficult it was going to be to break down the idea of the stint. We would like to think that if all teachers, and especially those of gifted children, realized that they are partly responsible for the existence of this limited approach, then they might take steps, as soon as the opportunity occurred, to prevent its development.

Another manifestation of under-achievement is boredom, but this is not always obvious to the class-teacher. In the course of discussion, we learned that most of these children were bored for some of the time, but they would not always have used that particular form of expression. Some of them declared that most of the work was too easy, but they did not necessarily show any great concern. One or two implied that school was tolerable because one met one's friends there but life really began at the end of the school day, either at home or outside. Most were keen on some form of sport or on the Cubs and Scouts, or on the Brownies, and they found an outlet for their energies there. Some found alternative employment in the classroom, like the girl who read quietly and extensively while the teacher was taking the class for a class lesson. Some were reconciled to the day in the class because they had never known any other conditions and assumed that their school lives were the norm. It should perhaps be pointed out again that all these children came from schools with large classes: in two or three cases the schools were really overcrowded and the buildings were far from modern. If they were working under cramped conditions during the day, several of these boys and girls were much more fortunate out of school, as they came from relatively spacious houses, where a play-room, or at least a room for play at suitable times, was readily available. Moreover, most of the children had their own little libraries and all belonged to a school or public library. In some of the homes there was ample provision of equipment so that several of the boys, in particular, were able to carry out some work in Science, even if it was only a system of inter-com between different rooms in the house. Several seemed to have the capacity to indulge in day-dreams or faraway thoughts and yet answer a question about the lesson even if it was suddenly addressed to them because they seemed to be paying little or no attention to what the teacher was doing or saying.

At first, when we set the children certain tests, some apparently suspected that we were merely repeating what they had had in school but at a somewhat different level. This was obviously a useful topic for a discussion which eventually proved very revealing. In the course of this discussion it became abundantly clear that these children were aware of the times in the classroom when the teacher was occupying them until other children had completed their work. The usual method was the giving of a lot of examples to be worked, or else some very hard examples. Some children felt that they were challenged, but others resented this technique as a waste of their time and effort. One boy put this view explicitly in pointing out that when he had worked two examples of some type of calculation he had been taught, then he understood the principle, so that further examples were a waste of time and a bore. We have since heard similar criticisms by gifted children in secondary schools about much of the homework they are set, a tradition, surely, that requires some informed re-assessment.

It has gradually become clear that if we accept the existence of under-achievement we must accept also that there are certain difficulties connected with the idea. First of all there is the need to work out some standard of achievement which one may expect from children, and this must be followed by the identification of those who are under-achieving. Our method of comparing work standards, reached by the children in their early days with us, with what we were able to reach with them after we had broken down the concept of the stint, was effective, but was possible only because we were dealing with small numbers of children who were of roughly the same intellectual ability. The process, even under the favourable conditions which we enjoyed, such as small numbers, homogeneity, time, skilled members of the staff and the removal of the children from their normal classroom atmosphere, was far from easy, so that without more favourable conditions and help from experienced people it seems unfair to expect a class-teacher with forty or more children to be able to undertake the process. It is possible of course, in some schools, to separate the children into groups or to use a system of assignments. This may make it possible to improve the situation, but there are two needs which must not be overlooked. One is the change in attitudes which will get rid of the "stint" approach, and this as far as we can see from our work requires some adult attention to these children, and, secondly, adult stimulation is required. Some people have suggested that all that is needed to cater for the gifted child is a good library to which he can be sent and encouraged to learn for himself. We doubt the efficacy of this solution, as, even when we tried this in a first-class children's library with resources much beyond those to be expected in any school, we found that the children failed to make full use of the facilities. The work produced was competent enough, but was disappointing by the standards we had hoped that they would achieve. On the other hand, when an assignment was set and an experienced teacher worked with the children, standards of achievement rose perceptibly. Alas! no teacher with other children to care for could find the time necessary to undertake this kind of stimulating work.

The shortage of time was high-lighted in another way, namely, in the amount of preparation required for an afternoon's work with such children. This might arise from the quantity of work of which the children are capable or from the quality. One student, who was very desirous of joining in with this work, following a voluntary trip with the children acting as escort, was assigned two boys, who were by no means outstanding on the WISC. Her main interest lay in Social Studies, and as soon as she knew that the boys were coming she mapped out a course to cover the first four weeks. Although she had the children for fifty minutes of each week, she found that her four-week course barely lasted the first period. The quality of the work was reasonable, but the quantity was insufficient, and so in the future she had to devote much more time to her preparation. Fortunately, she learned her lesson quickly and was able to apply this when later she taught, on teaching practice, the class from which one of the boys came. As for quality, tutors of the College, even when working in their own specialist fields, found that they had to prepare sometimes in a way which was more exacting than for their lectures to students. Several of the boys regularly read "Understanding Science" which was being published at the time in weekly parts, and their knowledge was surprisingly wide. They were, on the whole, less well versed in philosophy and literature, but their speed of understanding sometimes made an apparently adequate lesson suddenly seem all to easy. It is all too obvious that the teacher of a large class rarely if ever has the amount of time available to undertake the preparation required.

There is a problem here which requires attention and for which there are only a few possible solutions. One would be for a supernumerary teacher who might go from school to school taking groups of bright children and leaving work or suggested work with the regular class-teacher for the children to carry on with till the next visit. In days of teacher shortage this is hardly likely to prove feasible except in those fortunate areas to which teachers are strongly attached. Another possible method would be to accept the present situation as far as the daily class routine is concerned and to make provision outside the school, after school hours or on Saturday mornings: some groups of the National Association of Gifted Children have begun to have, or are contemplating, activity groups for such children on Saturdays, or at their annual camps. Whether this is adequate, in the sense that it will tend to alter the attitude of the children to the "stint," remains to be seen. Perhaps, if this solution is to be attempted—it is said to have been proved workable in the Soviet Union—the activities should be initiated by the local Education Authorities and put under their control.

A third possibility would obviously be to extend the kind of work which we have undertaken at Brentwood, bringing together children of roughly the same high ability at least once a week. It might well be tried out in a number of centres for a half-day or a day a week, either with special staff or with recognized good teachers seconded for a half-day or a day. Colleges of Education could co-operate directly by ensuring that students were available to help in those schools from which the teachers were seconded, and also by providing help and guidance to the teachers. Out of such work might well come the advice and help which the class-teachers of these gifted children require. Moreover, if such classes were sponsored by the local authorities, it would surely be possible for the class-teachers to have the opportunity from time to time to attend the groups, so that they would be able to see for themselves the work undertaken and the standards reached, to observe the behaviour of their pupils in different circumstances, and to contribute to discussions about the children and the work, from their personal knowledge of the children in the normal class-situation and also of the home background of the children.

Such groups might well lead to the transformation of attitudes and the development which we have come to consider as the great advantage of bringing together children of like ability. The first observable advantage was the smartening-up process which was soon visible in a number of cases. The children who were accustomed to a still more leisurely pace than the others in our groups, found that they were quickly left behind in any lessons which involved techniques such as question and answer. Especially in groups conducted by students, the classroom atmosphere of relative formality prevailed, and children raised their hands to answer. At first, partly because the children were drawn from different schools, so that there was a mild feeling of competition, and partly because the children in large classes were accustomed to indicate their readiness to answer, some of the children raised their hands promptly to give the answer. Other children knew the answer, but were less used to a quick response, and so they failed to put up their hands in time to be invited to give the answer. In the early days, much of the material was based on problems to which there was a definite answer, so that mostly the children responded in the wonted way. With College staff, on the other hand, the children tended to be treated as if they were in an adult group in which they were expected to speak or answer when they were ready without making any mechanical sign. Moreover, the work tended more and more to become "open-ended in nature" (more will be said of this in the next three or four chapters), which did not permit of any one definite answer. More reflection was required, and so a different technique of answering developed to correspond with this, and the earlier competitiveness gradually disappeared. Indeed the children began to listen more closely to the answers suggested by other children and they began to accept these answers as the bases of their own contributions. The speed of adaptation to this type of discursive answer varied considerably but it took place in all groups. The technical change was closely related to the change in quality of the discussion: it became possible for the teacher conducting a group to include statements which he knew required qualification, in the knowledge that some youngsters would promptly take the statement and point out its inadequacy. One boy in a later group, who recorded the highest score we have ever had on the full-scale of the WISC, and who attracted our visitors immediately by his well-groomed appearance in his white shirt, tie and shorts, was an outstanding example of what can be achieved. Referred to affectionately by some of the other gifted children as "Brains" (in the "Thunderbird" sense rather than in "Boss Cat") he was able to take an inadequate statement and discuss it with the cool detachment of a graduate discussing a matter with a fellow-graduate, in this case a tutor with an honours degree. Discussion at this level was extremely unlikely in any ordinary classroom and would not have been expected by ourselves until the older attitudes to work and teachers had been broken down.

Reference to our young professor in short trousers reminds us of one lesson which constantly obtruded itself upon us, and which seems of paramount importance, so that we are tempted to repeat it at frequent intervals. The lesson is that despite the high intelligence possessed by most of our children, and despite the high level of achievement of which the majority proved themselves capable, they were all still small boys and girls. This was made abundantly apparent as soon as they were released from the classroom for a break. If a boy had a ball with him, a game of football began in which there was the maximum expenditure of energy. The girls preferred to play more feminine games, while some of the boys not interested in football chased each other up and down the fire-escape. In these games, the fact that the children came from different schools was obscured much more completely than in the classrooms, where generally speaking the youngsters remained in their school groups whenever that was possible. We certainly learned as much about the character of the children at playtime as we did in the study-rooms. We feel that in any discussion of the problems of these children, and in any plans made to help them to a solution of those problems, the fact that they are small children and that they require contact with other children as well as with their intellectual peers, should be kept closely in mind. This is one reason for advocating a part-time scheme for providing contact with their intellectual peers, rather than the setting up of special schools or the permanent separation within the school, based on one factor only.

4 *Creativity*

S. A. BRIDGES, M.A., B.Sc., Ph.D.

OUR so-called Creativity Groups will be dealt with in the next two chapters, but the reasons for our entering into this field, and some of the preliminary work, will form the subject of the present chapter.

There were three main reasons for beginning work in this field. The first of these was our own conviction that high ability as measured by Intelligence Tests was only one form of giftedness and obviously there must be others; indeed, we had ample evidence in our own experience and from our reading that other gifts existed for which provision must be made in schools and in Colleges of Education. On the whole, Intelligence Tests seemed to favour certain forms of thinking and activity, and children who did not perform outstandingly on these tests often proved capable of a high standard of work in other directions. This conclusion was greatly strengthened by the evidence presented by Getzels and Jackson in their book *Creativity and Intelligence* [20]. Although their tests have been adversely criticized and their evidence has been assailed on statistical grounds, they brought out two points which seemed to be of value and which certainly merited further consideration. These findings were that creativity and intelligence seem to be at least partly independent of each other and that school-children who score more highly on creativity tests than on intelligence tests may have an equal scholastic attainment with those who score more highly on intelligence tests than on creativity tests. Now if their first finding is valid, and we have expressed it here in a qualified form, then this is of great importance to all concerned with education of children and with the training of teachers. The latter must be as carefully prepared for teaching the child with creative ability as for teaching the child with more commonly accepted abilities. Secondly, if the children with high creative ability tend to do as well in school as those with high I.Q.s, we must recognize that there are more factors involved than the abilities measured by our present intelligence tests. New approaches to teaching and to assessment of work become possible.

The second reason for undertaking work with children showing creative ability according to certain criteria (more fully discussed in the next chapter) was the widespread use of the word in the schools in which our students carried out their block teaching practice. In Infant Schools and Junior Schools our students were asked to be responsible for Creative Writing, Creative Dance, Creative Craft and so on. As a result of discussions with Head-teachers, class-teachers and our own students, we came to the conclusion that the word was being used in so many different ways that it had lost much of its original meaning. In many instances also the word was being used without adequate thought as to why it was being appended to a particular activity. Moreover, as we observed many of the activities and lessons which were labelled "creative," we could often see little evidence of any of the so-called attributes of creativity. All too often we failed to note any of the novelty, flexibility, fluidity or the high level of energy which we had come to expect from our studies in the literature on the subject. As a result of our observations and of our manifest inability to help our students to a proper appreciation of creativity and of creative work in schools, we decided to recruit a new group of children chosen in some way that might relate to creativity. As an aside it may be pointed out that the authorities from whose schools we obtained the children, and the students who volunteered to share in the work, seemed to favour this development rather than the further recruiting of children chosen on their high I.Q. scores.

The third reason for our study was the interest which we developed in what is really a fascinating literature on the subject. This literature was mainly American, and much of it dated from the late fifties when a new appreciation of the child with some gift developed, partly at least because of the rapid advancement of the U.S.S.R. in the field of Science. The bibliography will contain a list of the outstanding works; here, reference will be made to the works of four American writers and one dealing with English schoolboys. The first of these writers is J. P. Guilford [24], who from the early nineteen-fifties onward has tried to isolate the characteristics of creativity through factor analysis. He has devised a whole series of tests as the bases of his research. As a result of his factor analyses he claims to have isolated several factors, of which three of the most important are—

Sensitivity to problems as evidenced by an ability to see weaknesses or deficiencies and to suggest improvements.

The ability to see relationships which are not common— tests included the writing down of a number of ways in which objects are alike, and also the listing of unusual uses for common objects such as bricks, tin cans, etc. It is interesting to note that this ability to see relationships has often been regarded as one of the signs of high intelligence, but several writers would agree with Guilford that it is a characteristic or sign of creative ability.

Originality (one of the commonest attributes, sometimes referred to as novelty) as evidenced by an ability to supply clever captions for cartoons or clever titles for story plots, or, again, to write down a considerable number of synonyms for one word.

The second of the writers is E. P. Torrance [49], who seems to produce one book on the subject each year. He has been interested since the late fifties principally in the field of creativity assessments of school-children, and has developed the Minnesota Tests of Creativity. He has stressed the importance of measuring creativity in order that schooling may be made more efficient for each individual child and he has maintained that by ensuring the proper development of the mind, which includes creativity, adult behaviour will be improved and will be more predictable. The Minnesota Tests are of two types, the non-verbal (e.g., a circles test, in which each child is invited to make as many pictures out of 30 circles as he can in 10 minutes—we have used a similar test with six circles, but that will be referred to in the next two chapters), and the verbal, including guessing what has led up to and what may follow a scene shown in a picture, the improvement of a toy, and unusual uses of common objects, such as a tin can. The tests are then scored for flexibility, fluency, originality and elaboration, but they are very difficult to score, and Torrance himself acknowledges the limitations of his tests.

A third writer, C. W. Taylor [45, 46 and 47], has carried out studies at the University of Utah, but has been more concerned with adults, and especially interested in the field of Science. He has stressed the limitations of I.Q. tests which he maintains isolate far too few factors to be of much value in predicting achievement, far less creativity. He lays considerable weight, like Guilford, on divergent thinking as a factor in creativity—the divergent thinker, who is happiest in the fields of open-ended questions and problems, is the most likely person to show the attributes of creativity, such as fluency, flexibility and originality. Another characteristic is a sense of humour, which may reveal itself in a playfulness with ideas and words, which reminds me of the statement of Einstein that an ability to play with ideas is a sign of the mind which makes discoveries. Taylor also refers to a tendency towards a femininity of interests in the creative person: some other writers have agreed with Taylor and have suggested that the creative person finds difficulties in a society which tends to stress the "maleness" of the role of men and boys in society. Other writers, including Getzels and Jackson [20], have found that divergent thinkers are often less acceptable to school-teachers than are children who have a bias to convergent thinking or towards conformism.

Two other American writers merit a reference in passing, as they tried in two different ways to develop creativity as a team effort. The first of these was C. F. Osborn [40] who, in what he calls "brainstorming," encouraged groups to offer ideas without criticism or immediate evaluation, in the hope that valuable creative ideas would emerge. Later, W. J. Gordon [22], in his book *Synectics*, advocated a group of people from different disciplines meeting together to try to solve certain manufacturing problems, through bringing forward analogies in the various disciplines represented. For example, ideas from biology have been found to be applicable to commercial and other problems.

Before going on to deal with the fourth American work which has influenced us, this seems to be a suitable point at which to refer to one of the most fascinating books on creativity and intelligence, *Contrary Imaginations*, by Liam Hudson [29]. Hudson has studied bright secondary schoolboys in the Cambridge area, and as a result has come to certain conclusions, some of which are tentative. First of all, he has pointed out that when one is dealing with a class of clever boys, differences in I.Q. are not really important. Our evidence at Brentwood would not wholly support this affirmation, but there is some truth in it, and we shall keep this possibility in mind whenever we are planning work for intelligent or gifted children. Hudson looks at boys who show a bias towards convergent thinking or towards divergent thinking. After discussing the value of different kinds of test, he declares that he will call the "high I.Q." a "converger" and the "high creative" a "diverger." He reminds us, however, that there is a third category who are all-rounders, possessing the ability of both convergers and divergers. He reminds us also that a knowledge of children's scores on intelligence tests will not help us to guess their likely scores on open-ended tests and vice versa. As a result of work with his group, he has suggested that some 30 per cent of schoolboys are convergers, 30 per cent are divergers and 40 per cent are all-rounders. On such evidence as we have, from our work with our groups, we have no grounds for disputing these figures. Hudson has found that, on the whole, his arts specialists were relatively weak on the I.Q. tests but relatively strong on the open-ended tests, while most of his science specialists were strong on the I.Q. tests but relatively weak on the open-ended tests. Hudson, after considerable discussion, recognizes that original work may come from convergers as well as divergers, and he concludes that the differences are less those of the mind than of personality, which is greatly affected by conditioning and motivation. His work makes it clear that to date there has been insufficient study of both personality and creativity and that this is indeed a fascinating area of study.

The fourth American work, which has influenced our own work, is *Modes of Thinking in Young Children* by Kogan and Wallach [32]. As far as we are concerned, they have made three important contributions. Firstly, they have challenged the belief that creativity can be tested by group tests in the same way as intelligence: many critics of the latter would agree that tests, to be of any value, must be individual. Kogan and Wallach favour individual tests which are mainly oral in character, as they contend that only in such circumstances is genuine creativity likely to emerge. Secondly, they deal with four categories of children: those who score highly on tests of intelligence and of creativity, those who do not perform very well on either, those who score relatively highly on intelligence but not on creativity, and those who score relatively highly on creativity but not on intelligence. Thirdly, they suggest that as a result of their analysis and study of the children concerned, behaviour problems tend to arise, especially amongst boys, where the creativity score is much higher than that for intelligence.

Kogan and Wallach also suggested that there should be no special motivation in the case of creativity tests. In many tests, children are urged to produce as many ideas as possible or to put forward as many interesting ideas as possible, or to write as stimulatingly as they can. Such motivation may lead to an unnatural situation. It was with this admonition in mind that we approached one of our testing situations in preparation for work with our experimental groups. We tried out two tests on children who had just entered a secondary school and in both cases we were careful to avoid including any invitation to do their best, or to write interestingly, from the rubric. The two tests were verbal in nature and are described below.

The first of these tests was the writing of a story, consisting of a sentence or two, based on a group of words, which were carefully chosen so that one word at least would seem to be divergent. For example, there were five groups of four words with the following instructions—

"Look at the following four words: car, gun, man, boy. I am going to make up a little story using these four words—A *man* was sitting in a *car*. Presently he produced a *gun* and showed it to a *boy* who was standing beside the parking meter. Note that I have used each of the four words once only. Now you are going to have the chance of making up five stories, using each of the five sets of words below. Each story should be made up of two or three sentences. Now go ahead and try to make up your stories. Write your stories on this paper.

    1. shop, sky, sand, people
    3. fence, night, shorts, man
    5. car, medicine, ring, knife."

The reader will note that there was no deliberate encouraging stimulus to produce interesting or novel work either in the instructions or in the groups of words themselves.

A few examples will soon show that the response was normally quite uninspired—

"The sun in the sky was the colour of sand. The people in the shop were very busy."

"During the night a man in shorts climbed over the fence. He was a burglar."

"A car drew up and got our medicine. A man walked up the drive. There was a ring on the door. He came to see my brother who cut himself with a knife."

"I am with some people on the sand at Walton-on-the-Naze. The people that were with me said: Look at the beautiful sunny sky. Then they said, We are going to the shops."

"A man was walking through the night. He was wearing shorts, a hat and a shirt. He leaned over the fence and saw an object—it was a cow."

"There was a man who was a doctor who was going to take some medicine to a man who was ill. He had to ring the door-bell. He had a knife and gave it to the man as well as the other things he had to give. Then he drove off in his car."

"Five people came out of the shop. They went on to the sand where there was a helicopter. They got into it and soon it took them high up into the sky."

"One night a man jumped over the fence and stole some chickens. A boy who saw him told the police that the man was wearing a cap, a sports jacket and a pair of grey shorts."

"A man would not take his medicine and so he died. He left his son a car and a penknife. He left his wife a very valuable ruby ring."

These samples are probably sufficient to give a reasonable view of the responses, which varied considerably in quality. There were few stories from the 250 children who sat this test which made us feel that we were dealing with creative children. On the other hand, we must keep in mind that the test was carried out under normal conditions in a school, so that we may be experiencing again the idea of a stint; secondly, there was no special encouragement to do well; and, thirdly, these children were about eleven to twelve years of age, one of the two ages at which children seem to show less creative ability (and possibly less advance in intelligence).

The second test suggested by the work of Kogan and Wallach was the completion of a story, but as we were trying it out on some 270 children we were obliged to use it as a group test, despite the criticisms of Kogan and Wallach. As with these writers, we chose different stories, or rather, versions of the stories, for boys and girls, and we chose ideas from the field of defeat or where children were on the defensive. We shall give one story from the boys' paper and one from the girls' with two samples of the response in each case.

The instructions and the stimulus story for the boys were as follows—

Complete the following story—

"Oswald is in his first year of the secondary school. Things have gone badly for him since the first day. He has not done very well in his work and he knows that one or two of the teachers whom he likes think that he is rather thick. He never seems to think of the right answer in class when he is asked a question. He does not seem to get on very well with the other children. They make a fool of him in the classroom and also in the playground. When anything goes wrong, teachers and children seem to blame him. One day, he hears two boys talking about him: they say that nobody likes him and that he is of no use at anything. Oswald feels that he cannot put up with this any longer . . . ."

One boy was so depressed by this story that his conclusion was— "and so he went home as soon as school was over for the day and committed suicide."

Another boy wrote: "and so Oswald went to try to hit the two boys who were bigger than he was. The boys merely slipped off his trousers and gave him a beating. He was in despair, but afterwards he went home each night and did his homework, and each day he worked hard at school. He still did not have any friends and he often felt lonely and sorry for himself. One day they had a test, and Oswald sat by himself. All the boys made fun of him and said his brains would not work. He really tried hard and spent so long on one question that he never got them all done, but what he did do he got right. When the results came out, he was ninth out of thirty. The others were very surprised, as he usually came last. They stopped making fun of him, but when they had a game of football they would not let him play. So he practised and practised until he became best in the class, and so they let him play."

The ending shows a good deal of common sense, although the success at football may approach the more conventional fairy-story ending. It also shows a considerable measure of sympathy, which may well be an important factor in creativity. On the other hand, a boy not unlike Oswald in his early secondary experiences may well be writing from those actual experiences. More typical of the general response, and more conventional was the following—

"so that in the week-end Oswald thought about how he could improve. Then he had a brainwave and asked his Mum and Dad if he could join the library. They said, 'Of course you can!' Then he went up to the library in the town and said, 'Can I join the library?' She said, 'Here is your ticket; go and get your books.' So he kept going to the study-books and began to improve his school work, so that he got recommended lots of times."

The first of the stimulus stories for the girls and the instructions were as follows—

"On each side of this sheet there is the beginning of a story. Your job is to finish the story, telling us how the girl felt and what happened afterwards. Write your stories on this paper.

Emma Jane's Mother has always wanted her to be a wonderful dancer, and has sent her to dancing lessons. Emma Jane, however, is not very good at dancing; she can hardly keep time to the music. So, although she practises more than anyone else and tries her hardest, she has not done very well, and has never been asked to dance in any of the school shows. She knows that her Mother is very disappointed in her. She is disappointed herself, as she is really keen on dancing. At last she decides to give it one more try, and after she has practised a great deal she is given a chance to do a dance in the show put on by her dancing school. She is too anxious, however, to do well, and becomes nervous, trips and falls. She feels so upset that she bursts into tears in front of everybody. After the show, the dancing teacher tells her that she will never be any good as a dancer . . . ."

The majority of the girls, probably following the stories which are so common in the weekly magazines intended for pubescent and adolescent girls, ignored Emma Jane's fundamental weakness and made her an ultimate success in dancing, as in the following version—

"As she walked home she felt very sorry for herself. She saw her Mother running up the street to meet her. 'How did you get on, dear?' 'Not very well, I'm afraid,' and then she burst into tears. 'O Mother, I cannot dance and my teacher said so.' 'I'll go and see your teacher and ask if she will give you a second chance.' 'O Mother, will you?' Next day her Mother went to the teacher who said 'I'll give your daughter another chance.' Christmas soon came, and Emma Jane played as an angel. The people cheered her and applauded her at the end of the performance. Her Mother was very pleased. Now she is a great dancer and is very well known."

Some of the girls felt that the weaknesses of Emma Jane were so great that it would be foolish to think that they were likely to be overcome to such an extent that she could become an accomplished dancer, and that success should be sought by her in some alternative field. One of the better examples of this type of response is as under—

" 'We have never let you dance before, and because we let you, you messed up the whole show,' said Miss White.

Miss White was a very strict teacher and was really shouting at Emma Jane. It was not really Emma Jane's fault, as she had tripped on something that was on the stage. She was really very upset, and was more worried about her Mother and what she would think. 'She'll say that I am a clumsy good-for-nothing little girl,' Emma Jane was thinking to herself, as Miss White was walking away. Emma Jane really wanted to be a vet, as she loved animals although she also liked dancing. When her Mother came up to her Emma Jane said that she could not go on with the dancing, and told her that she really wanted be to a vet. And now she goes to the Vet's surgery every week-end and also every holiday that she gets."

There are several points arising from our use of these two tests. The first is that we were obliged to use them as paper tests, as individual testing was far beyond our resources. Moreover, as we have always hoped that our work might ultimately prove useful in schools, it is better that we should use techniques which can be used or adapted for use in schools. The second point is that although we regard tests of this kind as valuable, we were unable to make them a part of a proper battery, as has normally been done in any American experiment. The American testers are nearly unanimous in their stress on the fact that a battery of different tests should be used, as there are many factors or facets to consider.

The third point concerns the deliberate avoidance of specific stimulation in the rubric of the respective tests. There seems no case for this approach, as far as the test with the groups of words is concerned. A group of words seems itself to impose serious limitations although the words are of the simplest. The limitation is increased by the planned juxtaposition of words which do not readily suggest connections, such as shop and sand, medicine and ring, book and river. If a test of this type is to produce any really interesting material, then children require to be urged or cajoled into trying to make their story as interesting as possible. The test on the completion of the story is somewhat different. For quite a number of the boys and girls who sat their respective tests, the part of the story given them provided sufficient stimulation. This did seem to occur where the circumstances described in the story fitted in, in some measure, with their own experiences. In other cases this did not occur and so the children tended to regard this as merely another school chore requiring the production of two or three sentences. For such children, the attempt to stimulate interesting or original work would have to be made in the instructions. Such stimulation is unlikely to have the effect of interference which inevitably arises where tests are being applied orally and where such interference would vitiate the results.

The fourth point is that of assessment or interpretation of the material. This difficulty is common to all work which is to be assessed subjectively so that it is by no means new to teachers. In much assessment, some of the marks may be apportioned to the technical aspects which can be evaluated in a fairly objective manner. In the case of creativity tests we are not particularly concerned with the technical side, but we are trying to find evidence of a quality which cannot easily be defined. In some of the tests, help can be found in measuring quality as when children are asked to write down all the round things they can think of. In such tests some qualitative scoring can be undertaken by comparing lists and discounting those items which occur with a certain agreed frequency. Such techniques are difficult to apply to the story completion test, so that some other factor has to be considered. Kogan and Wallach try to solve this difficulty in certain instances by looking carefully at the actual content of the completion and attempting to decide how realistic the writer has been. If the writer has concluded, in face of all the facts to the contrary, that a boy is to become a successful athlete or a girl a successful dancer, by undertaking some more rigorous practice, then this is really a form of fantasy and so should not be rated highly. On the other hand, where the writer or his hero faces up to the unpleasant facts and seeks to succeed in some other field of activity, this is treated as realistic, and should be rated highly. This was the technique of evaluation which we used, although we realized that in some cases apparently hopeless failures do eventually succeed in a most unlikely activity because of a change in motivation. Our writers were probably too immature as psychologists to appreciate this and where they did follow this line it was probably the result of a need to have a happy ending.

Even where we used this agreed form of assessment, we found it difficult to apply, and it was extremely time-consuming. We felt, indeed, that if we ever wished to test fairly large numbers of children these techniques would require more time than we could possibly afford. We had already used the technique of an essay or composition with a divergent title, such as "The Flying Monkey," or "The dog that would not bark" as a part of a battery of tests to pick out our first Creativity group. Although the marking of this had presented problems, it was less demanding in time than some of these others and the results were no worse if they were not any better. In consequence, when we decided to screen some hundreds of junior schoolchildren as a first step towards choosing a second Creativity group, we decided to revert to the essay with the divergent title as the written part of the test. Once again, we have reason to think that, until something better is devised and tried out exhaustively, that type of test is as useful as any other. In addition to the written test there was a shapes test, and one that included responses to musical stimulation, but that testing programme will be dealt with in the course of the next two chapters.

5 *The Importance of Creativity as an Area of Study*

ANTHONY KINSEY, A.T.D.

E. PAUL TORRANCE, in *Education and the Creative Potential* [49 b], talking about American schools, says—

"One of the most revolutionary changes I foresee is a revision of the objectives of education. Today we proclaim that our schools exist for learning. We say we must get tougher and make our pupils learn more. Schools of the future will be designed not only for *learning* but for *thinking* . . . today's schools . . . are being asked to produce men and women who can think, who can make new scientific discoveries, who can find more adequate solutions to impelling world problems, who cannot be brainwashed, men and women who can adapt to change and maintain sanity in this age of acceleration. This is the creative challenge to education."

As in so many other activities, what is true of the U.S.A. is equally true in Europe. Something must be done to make our education system more meaningful in the context of modern problems and ideas. There are, of course, many points in the system which require radical revision, many attitudes which are in need of reappraisal, but certainly one of the most important is the realization of the existence of creative potential as a factor which is not necessarily synonymous with intelligence as it is traditionally measured. Too long we have rewarded convergent intelligence at the expense of creative intelligence. Our truly creative individuals have emerged largely in spite of, rather than as a result of, the education they have received, and this is as true of creative engineers and scientists as of practitioners in the arts.

One should, I suppose, begin any serious discussion of the subject of creativity with an attempt at a definition. The *Concise Oxford Dictionary* is not very helpful: it deals with the word "create"— bring into existence; give use to; originate—it mentions "creative," "creatively," and "creativeness," but ignores completely "creativity." Perhaps there is no such word. Glancing down the dictionary page, by-passing "creatine" (an organic base found in the juice of flesh) we come to "creation"—act of creating; a production of the human (esp. dressmakers, actors) intelligence, esp. of the imagination. As I say, not really very helpful, but suggesting some key words like "intelligence" and "imagination."

Obviously no concise definition is possible. The best we can hope to do is to bring together some of the ideas engendered by the word "creativity" and allow them to act as a frame of reference throughout our discussion. What, for example, do we mean by a creative person? Possibly a person who can react to a problem or a set of circumstances in an original and personal manner, so as to produce a conclusion which is both logical and unexpected. This again is only a partial definition, making no allowance for that aspect of a creative production which satisfies an aesthetic.

On the other hand, if we are not too sure what we mean by "creative," we can be very certain as to what we do not mean. If one were asked to suggest a word that was currently so overworked as to lose all meaning, "creative" could very easily be that word. Pick up any journal concerned with general education and in it one will find endless advertisements for books on creative this and that, from Needlework to Mathematics. Unfortunately the majority of such books have nothing whatever to do with real creativity in the sense that we use the term, but simply provide the children with a number of ideas devised by adult ingenuity.

Likewise, many of the activities carried on in schools under the heading of creative work have very little truly creative content. Activities such as sticking milk straws together to make decorative Christmas stars, etc., provide children with virtually nothing in the way of creative experience, the products of such activities being both adult-orientated and predictable.

On the contrary, we are concerned with discussing the child's innate ability to produce an original response to a stimulus which is at the same time child-centred and open-minded.

There are two questions which need to be answered. Firstly, is there a separate factor in human intelligence to which we can apply the term "creativity"? Secondly, at what age can such a factor be distinguished, and how best can it be developed and encouraged? There are also a number of subsidiary questions, such as, to what extent is "creative" just another term for "divergent"? Is it possible to *train* as distinct from *encourage* creativeness? In other words, is it possible to make an apparently uncreative person creative, and conversely, can a creative spirit be deadened by unsympathetic teaching?

I think there is some misunderstanding arising from the first question. Because of the recent increasing interest shown in creativity, it is often thought that creativity is some completely new quality which has only just been discovered, like some new planet, and that it is in some way extra to intelligence. The fact is that creative ability is and always has been part of intelligence, i.e., the mental competence of a human being, but has until comparatively recently been ignored both by traditional intelligence-testing techniques and by educational processes.

It is not so much the discovery of creativity which is new but the discovery that traditional tests of intelligence, on which so many of our selection processes have been based, have largely ignored this important aspect of human performance, that has brought a new light to bear on the whole subject.

Some of the earliest studies of creativity took place as long ago as the beginning of this century, but on the whole these were isolated pieces of work, outside the main stream of psychological research. The main body of literature on this subject has been produced in the U.S.A. since the late 1950s and has been motivated by the concern of the U.S. government to find ways of educating creative scientists for subsequent employment in commercial—industrial and military—industrial fields. Whatever the motivation may have been, the fact is that many American universities have conducted extensive research into the problems of testing for and educating creativity, and the resulting literature is now very extensive and sufficiently complete to enable us to form some fairly firm conclusions.

It would be presumptuous to attempt a fully comprehensive summary of all this mass of material in these few pages. Although there are inevitably some contradictions in detail, most of the American studies support one another on the major issues, and certain basic points emerge which have been of value to us in the conduct of our own modest programme. Readers who wish to consult the original material may find the bibliography, included at the end of this book, helpful.

Most of the American research has been concerned with adults or children of Junior-high or High-school level, that is, over the age of 11+, although some writers on individual subject areas, like Viktor Lowenfeld [35], whose main concern is with art education, provide some relevant material from work with younger children.

The first point to arise, which seems to be of vital interest, is the indisputable fact, resulting from extensive and very thorough testing, that it is possible to divide the more able children into two groups, both of which are equally successful in their school performance, but which are very unequal in terms of measured intelligence. The high I.Q. group (I.Q. measured by traditional techniques) exhibit the achievement expected of such a group. The other group, whose I.Q.s are as much as 20 points lower, appear from the school records to be over-achievers. When both groups are tested for creative potential, a test that is not usually administered in the normal school situation, it is found that the second group produce much higher scores than the first or conventionally high-intelligence group (Getzels and Jackson [20]).

This is probably a simplification, and other researchers, notably Kogan and Wallach [32], find other and more complex divisions and groupings as a result of rather more sophisticated techniques for testing creativity potential.

The conclusions to be drawn, however, seem to be fairly clear, namely that the highly creative child is usually of above average general intelligence but rarely at the very top in this respect. It is also observable that in terms of actual scholastic performance the highly creative child is generally equal to his more conventionally intelligent colleague. This in spite of the fact that the school situation in which he is expected to compete generally favours the convergent (high I.Q.) rather than the divergent (high creativity) thinker.

It would also seem, for reasons that are too complex to go into here, that the creative child gets less positive support from his home background than the high-I.Q. child, which must also be a factor working against the creative child (Getzels and Jackson [20]).

Two other indications emerging from the American studies are not in themselves crucial to the understanding of creativity as such, but are of interest in any consideration of the way in which a creative child should be treated in school. Firstly, it seems that the creative child has a more highly developed sense of humour. In very many cases when high-intelligence and high-creativity children were presented with the problem of providing an explanation for a given set of circumstances, or completing a story, the offerings of the creative children were not only more original and unexpected but were also highly amusing, even witty. An illustration of the two different approaches can be found by reference to one of the studies carried out by Getzels and Jackson [20]: two adolescents being tested were presented with a picture stimulus of a man at ease in a passenger aircraft. The high-I.Q. student gave an orthodox account of a successful business man looking forward to being re-united with his family. On the other hand, the high-creativity student saw the man as one who had just divorced his wife on the grounds that she had used a face-cream which made her skid dangerously in the marital bed, and who was now thinking in terms of inventing a new, less dangerous face-cream. One student wrote seriously, the other with his tongue in his cheek.

Secondly the studies suggest that the creative child tends to show a marked interest in the kinds of activities traditionally associated with the opposite sex. Boys show an interest in dressmaking, cooking, dolls' houses, etc.; girls, in mechanical problems, etc. Superficially this could be taken to suggest that creative boys are effeminate and vice versa. In fact the explanation would seem to me to be much more straightforward and hold certain implications for the modification of our educational system, namely that the creative child is: (a) more interested in every aspect of his world, regardless of what is traditionally expected of him; and (b) is prepared to break through artificial and imposed subject barriers.

If this is indeed true, it means that much of what we regard as right and proper treatment of the different sexes in the school situation must be radically revised if we are to provide the most stimulating education for the creative child.

6 *An Account of the Experiment*

ANTHONY KINSEY, A.T.D.

VERY few Colleges of Education are staffed or equipped to carry out detailed and comprehensive experiments on the lines of those conducted by American Universities. The prime function of a College of Education is to train teachers and any experimental work that is attempted in such an establishment must of necessity be supplementary to this basic function. Lecturing staff are all fully occupied with their day-to-day tutorial duties and all research must be fitted into an already full time-table; also, any work of this nature must be fully integrated into the existing College course. There are no graduate students available to act as research assistants. The students involved are all inexperienced in handling and understanding children, and however carefully one structures a research project involving the study of children, much of the evidence emerging from such a project is of a kind that requires an almost intuitive understanding that only comes from years of contact with children.

Having already established in the College a programme to study children of very high intelligence, it seemed logical to start a small pilot project to investigate the hitherto neglected subject of creativity, using a group of children drawn from the same local Primary Schools.

It could be argued that the most obvious way to investigate creative potential would be to take a team of staff and students into schools to work with groups of unselected children in their normal environment, but, having established the idea of bringing selected children into the College to work, it was decided that to begin with, at any rate, the same general procedure should be followed. Assuming we could select on the basis of creative potential, and that the selected children did prove in practice to possess above-average creativity, any work we did with them would be at a higher creative level and would provide us with a much clearer indication of the sort of qualities we were dealing with than would be observable with a group of children of mixed ability.

Ideally, of course, we would have liked to be able to operate a control group, a normal class of the same age as our selected group in one or other of the contributory schools. The control group could have been provided with similar tasks and activities to the College group, and any significant variations in performance recorded. We decided, however, that since at this stage our objectives were undefined and that we were not really engaging upon a truly scientific experiment, but simply a piece of open-ended investigation, we would dispense with the luxury of a control group. At a much later stage, some of the students did go into schools to try out some of the activities we had devised during the programme, but without any very conclusive results.

The more one works with children in an experimental situation the more one realizes how impossible it is to produce conclusions which are easily susceptible to analysis. There are so many elements over which one has absolutely no control. To start with, one is dealing with two sexes, both of whom have different characteristics and whose stages of development do not coincide. In an area like Essex, family backgrounds are almost infinitely variable. Children in school are subjected to a multitude of different educational approaches and influences, not only from school to school but also from class to class and teacher to teacher.

For example, one of the schools from which some of our children were eventually selected was of a very formal nature with an emphasis on academic work and a record of 11+ "successes" of which the headmaster was very proud. The other school which provided a large proportion of our first "creative" group was of the opposite kind, and placed an emphasis on project work, music and drama.

We were forced by all these considerations to the conclusion that the most important thing to do was to begin; that is, to gather together a group of children, a number of members of staff and some students. We held a meeting or two of the staff who showed an interest in the project and it became clear that there were to be, from the outset, a number of areas of disagreement. Some measure of disagreement is inevitable in a discussion of a subject as unexplored and as misunderstood as creativity, but the depth and extent of the disagreement became fully evident only in the first few weeks of work with the children. This will be referred to later.

My own point of view regarding the object of the experiment was fairly clear, namely, to find out what one could about the creative thinking process and explore ways in which creative thinking can be stimulated in a classroom situation. I did not and do not believe that in our particular College situation we could begin to compete with the Americans in terms of pure scientific research. But by approaching the subject with an open mind, by being prepared to accept negative as well as positive results, we might eventually produce a body of experience which could be of value in restructuring the approach to Primary education with an eye on the needs of the creative as well as the intelligent (in terms of traditionally measured intelligence) child.

If, as I have implied earlier, much contemporary education, with its emphasis on factual learning, favours the convergent child, what kinds of activity most encourage creative thinking?

The other function of the experiment, bearing in mind the nature of the College, would be to involve a number of students in the work so that they too could benefit from this first-hand experience with children of this kind.

Having decided to work with a group of children in the College, the first task was to set about selecting the children. We required fifteen to twenty children, to be drawn from the third-year groups in two of the local Primary Schools. What selection procedure could be used? There is very little test material available with an emphasis on the creative aspect of a child's performance. As Kogan and Wallach [32] have demonstrated, testing for creative potential is never an easy process and requires individual supervision and unlimited time, in order that the full potential of each child tested can be realized.

We also, in those early days, made the mistake of associating creativity almost exclusively with performance in the traditional aesthetic subjects—creative writing, music, visual arts, dance, etc.

This rather limited our approach, but in a sense counterbalanced the American research, which has been heavily weighted on the side of creativity in science subjects. Indeed, it is generally recognized that the main impetus, financial and otherwise, behind the extensive research into this whole subject in American universities, has resulted from the realization of the need to produce creative scientists in both the industrial and military fields.

Our instinctive concern with the arts when discussing creativity is probably a reflection of the English cultural tradition, which makes a clear division between, on the one hand, the practical and useful, which we tend to associate with intellect, and, on the other, aesthetics, which we somehow associate with intuition and creativity. This attitude will not, of course, bear serious examination, but still affects the thinking in a very large number of educational establishments.

The test procedure we adopted was first to ask all the children in the year groups to be tested to write an essay with a divergent title, and to list unusual uses for an everyday object, like a tin can. This gave us some indication of a child's ability in written English and distinguished the children who had a tendency to think divergently. In fact, evidence of the latter capacity affected our decision to select a particular child more than any other consideration.

The second part of the exercise consisted of certain members of the Music, Art and Physical Education Departments of the College visiting the schools and giving short tests in those particular subjects, either to children individually or in class groups. To use the word "test" in this context is not strictly accurate, as no self-respecting art teacher would consider testing children in art. What happened in fact was that the children were given two pieces of work to do which, we hoped, would give some indication of each child's originality or divergency and his powers of perception and general sensitivity in visual matters. We were, of course, also working on the assumption that some children whose lack of ability in written English might inhibit their performance in the written test might perhaps find a more sympathetic area of expression in visual art.

In the first of these two tasks we provided the children with an extensive selection of natural objects—shells, feathers, pebbles, etc., from which each child was asked to select the one which particularly caught his or her fancy. He was then asked to study it, draw it, paint it, or, if he felt like it, write about it. The supervising staff observed and made notes about the children while they worked, answered questions about the objects, noting at the same time any particularly interesting or original questions and the children who asked them.

When most of the children had exhausted the possibilities of this particular activity, the class was given a few minutes' break and then presented with another task. This time, the children were asked to draw or paint a picture of either their mother or father in a fairly typical situation, e.g., in the kitchen or working in the garden—not in itself a particularly original subject, but one to which most children could be expected to respond and which provided the supervising staff with both a clear idea of the developmental level of the individual children and some indication of their capacity to respond visually to their environment. The results of this task would also indicate which, if any, of the children were non-visual or haptic* in their thinking processes.

The end product of all these tests was a group of about 18 boys and girls who, in one way or another, showed themselves to be more original or divergent than their fellows. I must stress again the subjective nature of this selection process and that we were concerned with producing a group of children with whom we could work, and that no attempt was made to differentiate between the children within the group. At a later stage the selected children were tested for intelligence and proved to have I.Q.s ranging from 120 to, in one instance, 157 (in this respect our group proved to be very similar to the "high creative" children in the Getzels and Jackson experiment [20]).

Having selected the children, we had to decide on the form of the experiment. This presented a number of difficulties initially. As soon as one tries to combine the activities of a number of different teachers or tutors, each with his or her own specialist subject interest, one comes up against the problems of reconciling

* Concerned with touch.

the different objectives and approaches contained in those subjects, and this provided something of a stumbling block in the first few weeks of work with the children. The idea of each interested tutor operating with the group of children in turn, watched by the small group of students who had demonstrated an interest in this experiment as a basis for their extended course work, soon foundered in practice. The afternoon's activities became nothing more than a series of demonstration lessons which, however well done, did not provide a particularly creative experience for the children.

Quite soon this approach was abandoned and the work allotted to the students with one tutor, myself, as general supervisor.

It was decided to divide the children into small groups each of which was to work under two students, paired up on the basis of their special interests and abilities, and this form was kept for the duration of the experiment. The brief given to the students was very simple and was as follows. "Given that the children you are working with are reasonably intelligent, possibly divergent (the problems of defining creativity were fully discussed), what activities can you devise within your own special interests and abilities which will provide a stimulus for these children which is, if possible, outside the general run of activities normally available in the school situation?"

The students were also encouraged to think of themselves as leaders within the group, initiating activities but always being ready to respond to suggestions from the children. We realized that this is indeed a very difficult role to play for a person inexperienced in the ways of children, as most of our group of students were, and in practice we found that the students had some difficulty in creating an atmosphere of organized informality within their groups. If they learned nothing else, they did learn how difficult it is to break away from the traditional teacher-pupil relationship, not only from their own standpoint as teachers but also from the standpoint of the children whose experience leads them to expect the adult to be somewhat dictatorial in his handling of a class. The numerical ratio between pupils and students was largely dictated by the numbers of both available, but on average worked out at two students to a group of five or six children. We operated this arrangement throughout the duration of the first two-year experiment, but the consensus of opinion in the end was that the groups were really rather too small to form fully self-stimulating units and the students felt that they became rather isolated from their fellows working with other groups in different rooms. In other words, the experiment became somewhat fragmented. A technique had to be devised for recording results, and this presented several problems. We had stressed to the students at the outset that they were not to place too much emphasis on the tangible end products of a particular activity and that their main function was not so much to produce exhibition material as to involve the children thoroughly in the activities which they had devised: that in work of this kind the educational value of a project often consisted in apparently insignificant happenings during the progress of the project. With this in mind, the students were advised to pay attention to and, if possible, record things like the conversations overheard between individual children whilst they were working, particularly if the conversation threw any light on a child's reaction to the task on which he was engaged or on his thinking process.

Recording the progress of a project or activity, including the meaningful trivia, required some easily workable system. Obviously children would react unfavourably to someone hovering over them the whole time with a notebook, so at the risk of omitting some of the detail it was decided that as far as possible notes should be written up immediately the children had been dismissed. They were written on a specially duplicated form which was simply headed with the date, the number of the group and the names of the students conducting the particular activity. In theory, these record sheets could be collected together at appropriate times during the course of the experiment and the information collated. In practice, in the hurly-burly of the experiment, the sheets became neglected, and we were forced to the conclusion that the permanent stationing of a student "recording angel" in a room throughout the afternoon was an unavoidable necessity.

The selection of activities was deliberately left to the discretion of the students, with staff providing help and guidance when required. It was hoped that activities would range from those normally experienced in school, which could, in a way, act as control activities to show whether or not our chosen children would habitually produce exceptional work under normal classroom conditions, to highly original activities like making animated films.

It would be impossible to record here systematically all the activities which engaged the children on the first experiment, but the following can be taken as representative—

1. *Picture-making, Exploiting Different Media*

In this activity the basic stimulation was probably similar to that experienced by the children in their usual school art periods. The "extra" that we tried to introduce consisted in the use of different, and from the children's point of view unusual, media or scale of work.

2. *Objective Drawing and Painting*

This consisted of providing the children with interesting natural objects (a deer's skull, for example), or live animals—rabbits, guinea pigs—and asking them to draw, paint or write about their chosen object. We always spent some time discussing the object in detail with the children at the beginning of the period, not only its appearance but also its origins, history, etc.—in other words, anything which would help the children to identify with the object. In this preliminary discussion, the children were encouraged to contribute on an equal footing with the students conducting the discussion, and the students were expected to note any particularly interesting or significant comment coming from any of the children. The most usual form of expression finally chosen by the children was drawing or painting although many of them added written comments to their work.

I was particularly interested in this aspect of the experiment as I have always felt that the view commonly held, that children of this age are not capable of objective observation, is an over-simplification, and that most children can enjoy drawing objectively and can demonstrate very keen powers of observation (the extreme haptic child is probably an exception here, but there seemed to be no children of that nature in our particular group).

3. *Work Concerned with Dramatic Expression*

Mask making and the creation of characters led to simple mime plays. Some students, whose own specialist interests were in the dance-movement area, introduced a certain amount of work involving movement to music, but largely through lack of experience on the students' part this activity was presented in a rather formal manner, and, although the children entered into the spirit of the thing with complete lack of self-consciousness, little of original or creative merit emerged, and the students decided to find other material for their extended course work.

4. *The Use of Scrap Material*

From the point of view of discovering the degree of invention of our children, this was probably the most successful exercise. For this activity we gathered all the children together and presented them with a whole room full of scrap material of one kind or another, which we had collected together over a number of weeks. This material ranged from quite sizeable cardboard cartons to wood shavings and small off-cuts of timber; there were also fabric pieces, egg cartons, plastic packing material, in short, anything which could be cut, sawn, glued, Sellotaped, stapled or tied together. Undoubtedly the children from at least one of the schools had worked with material of this nature before, but certainly never on such a scale or under such favourable conditions. We also provided a wide range of tools, glues, etc., and began the afternoon's activity by giving the children very clear and detailed instructions in their use. Beyond that we said very little, other than that we hoped every child would use the materials provided to construct any object suggested by the materials. If the children preferred to work with colleagues, this was perfectly acceptable and in the event many of them did so.

The stimulus was to come from the material itself and the ingenuity shown by the children, both in their selection of material and means of construction, was quite remarkable. Also, the range of objects created was very considerable and indicative of the kind of thinking natural to the individual children. An examination of this particular experiment in detail could occupy a complete chapter. Sufficient to say that more than any other activity it provided an insight into the mental processes, levels of development and background of our children.

5. Work with Clay

The students working in this area were mainly pottery students and their approach tended to be rather traditional. However, there were times when the children were encouraged to be experimental and produce work of an individual nature.

6. Using Materials and Equipment not Normally Available in Schools

Examples were, putting over a story in sound on a tape-recorder, or making short sequences of 8 mm. animated film.

There was, throughout, an emphasis on activities normally associated with Art and Craft. This was due, I think, not so much to the fact that this is my own specialism and that the children were working in the College Art and Craft studios, as to the fact that the students who opted to take part in this experiment, as part of their extended course work, were and have been mostly main Art students. One could also argue, I suppose, that some of the less restrictive work takes place in a normal school situation and therefore any practical experiment in divergent thinking would tend to turn in this direction. My view is that any future experiment would benefit from less emphasis on the visual art side and more emphasis on literary and scientific work. This we have indeed tried to accomplish in more recent experiments with a newly selected group of children.

I have used the word "experiment" throughout the description of our work with these children, but I would hope that the reader would not interpret the word too literally. May I re-emphasize that there was very little of a truly scientific nature about the activities in which we were engaged, in the sense that as a result of the three years' work we are now in a position to make confident statements about the creative thinking of seven- to ten-year-old children. Our aim was to provide a particular group of children with stimulus activities which would allow the creative child scope to demonstrate his powers of invention, ingenuity, creativity, divergency, call it what you will. We aimed to make every task an open-ended one, without any pre-determined solution. Obviously, even the comparatively inexperienced students had some idea before they started a particular project as to what might emerge at the end. No teacher can provide a starting point without some expectation that a development is possible. What we tried to instil into our students was the realization that they must be prepared for any solution that the children might provide, however much this might diverge from the original ideas of the students themselves.

What conclusions can one draw from the progress of the experiment so far as it has gone? "Conclusions" is probably much too strong a word and we must content ourselves with one or two pointers and indications, none of which, one must confess, would stand up to the rigorous examination usually expected from the educational psychologist, but which may, if taken in the spirit of toleration, provide something of a guide for further action in both the experimental field and the classroom.

Firstly, what is the value of an experiment in creative aptitude with children of the age of seven or eight? Our work seems to suggest that if one can talk about a "creative" type he is not easily distinguishable at this young age. The kind of activities of which a seven-year-old is capable and in which he can be interested are, perhaps, not sufficiently complex to permit of much distinction between one child and another. Obviously, the older a child becomes the more experiences he absorbs and the more possibilities there are for gauging divergency. I suppose one could liken the situation to that of trains leaving a station on different tracks; the farther they go the more distant they become from one another and the easier it is to determine not only the lateral distance along the track but also the angular distance between the tracks.

But saying that it is not easy to distinguish in terms of creativity between one child and another is not the same as saying that children of this age are not creative and do not respond to a creative stimulus. Quite the contrary. Our experience was that the creative content of the work produced, and the degree of involvement of the children, was at times of a very high order and seemed to be in direct proportion to the creative potential of the starting point or stimulus that was provided.

When the children were provided with, say, a run-of-the-mill picture-making subject, of the kind they would almost certainly have been given in their normal school situation, their response was almost invariably less intense than when they were provided with an activity or starting point which contained a little more challenge, such as the use of new materials.

The reader may claim, with some justice, that this state of affairs could be expected and that obviously, if the class-teacher had time and energy to be constantly devising new ideas to present to the children, their involvement would be increased. But it is not quite as simple as that. To begin with, we have the well-recognized phenomenon of the child liking what he knows and repeating previous successes, particularly in the area of the visual arts. One would have expected this to show itself in our work with the children.

Secondly, in our experiment, although we were working with somewhat smaller numbers than the teacher could expect in a classroom, the physical conditions of work were no more satisfactory, and for much, although not all of the experiment we were at pains not to provide materials or equipment which were too far outside the range of those normally available to the class-teacher.

What we did in fact try to do was to increase the creative potential of an activity, in terms which a child of that age could appreciate. To the mature adult, particularly if he is experienced in the medium he is working in, almost any subject or starting point is so full of potential that the difficulty lies in selection and elimination. Indeed, one of the chief barriers that the adult has to cross, when placed in a situation in which he is expected to be creative on a given theme, is that of selecting his approach and not being confused and distracted by other possibilities.

This seems to be much less true of the young child, and our experience would suggest that if his starting point is sufficiently stimulating he has much less difficulty in deciding the direction in which his invention should carry him. One of the characteristics possessed by most of our children was that of almost immediate commitment to an idea, which was held to throughout the time allotted to the activity.

Our students also discovered that it seemed to be characteristic of creative children to be more self-contained within their own productive activity and less liable to be distracted by the activities of their neighbours.

None of the observations we made were particularly new, but one of the prime functions of an exercise of this kind is not so much to produce new material as to provide student teachers—as distinct from students of psychology—with first-hand experience of observing certain tendencies in operation. For example, I am sure that our students could have learned much from observing another characteristic of children of this age, which may in some way be connected with their ability to work without distraction, namely, their inability to combine with others without considerable loss of creative content. The old axiom, "two heads are better than one," does not, it seems, apply to children of seven or eight, or before the "gang" age.

It was very noticeable that in mime activities the invention shown by individual children, when invited to mime a particular theme, was far superior to that shown in a group effort. The latter invariably seemed to result in an exhibition of the lowest common denominator of the imagination of the group. To a lesser extent, the same phenomenon was observable when two children worked together on, say, a construction project or a tape-recording activity. In these cases, one of the two children would appear to dominate the activity, with the second child acting as an assistant or "labourer."

From this kind of observation, one hopes, the student will learn, from first-hand experience, how careful one has to be when planning group work with children of this age; that even group project work, other than that in which the teacher plays the dominant part with the children as helpers (which is probably of little value anyway) is perhaps not really possible at this age.

But I would say that by far the most important lesson to be learned by our students, from participation in this experiment, is that in teaching one just cannot talk glibly about results in terms of tangible, material evidence—a fact which puts one in a very difficult position when writing this account. To say that such and such an activity was successful, because it produced a goodly number of models or pictures or whatever, which could be exhibited in the classroom, is simply nonsense. One has to look much deeper to find the true value of a classroom activity; one has to learn that a full classroom display may, *or may not*, indicate that something really worth while is happening at child level. The lesson that our students need to learn, above all others, is that one can really appreciate how much success one is having as a teacher only by developing a kind of invisible antenna which can be tuned in to every little happening in the class: the expression on a child's face, the overheard snatch of conversation, the degree of involvement with which a child is working.

There is a sense in which teaching becomes an almost intuitive response to the needs of an individual in a group situation. If the particular need of an individual is to be allowed to be creative, the teacher must himself understand the nature of creativity in so far as this is possible. He must also realize that creative activity does not of necessity produce a tangible product, that it is what is happening within the child—the process, not the product—that has real meaning and significance.

These are some of the lessons that we hope our students learned from their experience with "creative" children.

7 A Non-specialist Approach to a Group of High I.Q. Children

PATRICIA MELDON, B.Sc., M.A., Ph.D.

It seems best to begin by clarifying the title of this chapter—in particular the use of the expression "a non-specialist approach." I chose to deal with a new group of Junior children recruited from Havering, as a general practitioner; and this was done because as a Primary teacher, both by training and inclination, I am still very much aware that most Primary teachers are burdened by large numbers, all day and every day, and the crucial question seems to be, what do we do with such children in the normal hurley-burley of the classroom?

With this in mind, we undertook fairly routine things: potential group activities within a larger class, using resources which are generally available. Some of the usual Junior-school topics were explored, in depth, and with as much detail as seemed appropriate; and these included much discussion and freedom of choice, beginning with constructive toys such as Meccano and bricks. It must be remembered that on arrival the average age of the group was only nine; that these youngsters were still children.

I wanted to know if and how they tackled such activities differently from the less able, in the hope that some conclusions would emerge which might be relevant to ordinary classroom practice. I suspect that, whatever we have gained from an objective and privileged study has been the philosophy of perceptive teachers for many years; the dilemma lies in being able to apply in practice what one knows and believes in theory.

There are certain other qualifying statements which must also be admitted: the first one will be familiar to experienced researchers.

Firstly, it was difficult to conceal from the children the fact that they were, in some ways, a selected group. On the strength of increased acquaintance I did once ask them if they knew why they came to the College, and from various sources they had adduced the reasons that they were brighter than average, and were helping with some experimental work. When any group knows that it is the subject of special study, then it tends to rise to the occasion, and there is added motivation to do well. There was also some advantage in discussing this with them, because they then felt that they were co-operating partners rather than experimental "guinea-pigs."

Secondly, there were no serious attempts at rigorous research; no hypotheses were made explicit, and no tests were made for statistical significance. These initial studies were therefore mainly exploratory.

A third possible qualifying statement could arise from the fact that the teacher-pupil ratio in this group was approximately one teacher to four children. In the case of the students who also worked with them, this would imply one novice teacher to a tiny handful of children, but the ratio was still disproportionately high. When asked directly, the latter said that they preferred to be with College staff; this was probably an exercise in discretion, however, rather than a sign of any real discrimination, since they worked with very capable mature students.

This potential for tact and insight, which will be referred to again later, is thought to be a function of their intellectual maturity; yet outwardly these children were normal, ebullient, egocentric Juniors. They had their minor squabbles over such things as who should have the best seat in the coach; and they were not above throwing around the loose coke which they found in the College grounds, or disappearing into the woods for a prolonged playtime.

The group originally totalled thirteen—6 girls and 7 boys— with scores on the WISC ranging from 122 to 153; and they were found to conform to the favourable profile of intellectually gifted children as described by Terman [48] over forty years ago. They were physically appealing, neither prone to being puny nor possessed of bulging foreheads and glasses like pebbles. They were not over-specialized in their abilities and interests, or emotionally unstable; and with their peers, at least, not socially unadaptable. They were generally spruce in their immaculate school uniforms, and had an overall air of alertness and vitality.

Their range of interests was evidenced by the extra-curricular activities they pursued, and the width of their reading. Avid reading is natural to such children, and is an activity which they enjoy with innocent single-mindedness. A girl was missing one Friday afternoon when the coach was ready to take them home, and she was found in the library, tucked away behind one of the shelves. She was nearly in tears when she realized that the coach had been kept waiting.

In accordance with the now generally accepted notion that intelligent children are potential all-rounders, their activities included team games, sports, swimming, Cubs and Brownies, musical instruments such as recorders and piano, drama, fossil-hunting, natural history, electronics, astronomy, and many others. Two of the girls enjoyed horse-riding, and they were all noticeably compassionate on the subject of animals generally.

Their common interest in reading ranged from Enid Blyton to scientific non-fiction, and their favourite books were currently historical novels, books on sport (which included ponies), tales of real-life heroes, and animal stories. Their enjoyment of the Paddington books in particular served to remind one, yet again, that they were also typical Primary children. Yet, they seem able to entertain discrete interests, such as a liking for dolls, and an appreciation of Chaucer at one and the same time.

This tolerance for disparate ideas was certainly characteristic of the group described here; and, if it can be assumed to be a generalized trait of the intellectually gifted child, it is probably irritating to adults and therefore misleading. It seems appropriate, therefore, to discuss now certain personality attributes which emerged, again suggestive of dissonance, but relevant to this general description of the children's characteristics.

Once the group had settled in, two personality tests were introduced: the Junior Eysenck Personality Inventory, and a modified version of the Myers-Briggs Type Indicator [39]. These are, respectively, British and American questionnaires, based on Jung's concepts of introversion and extraversion as dimensions of personality. Both instruments rely on self report: that is, the declared preferences of subjects; and, although they are no substitutes for informed judgments, perhaps such tests do provide an empirical foundation for statements which would otherwise be too speculative.

The idea that intelligence and introversion are correlated has some appeal: reading, for example, which is a cognitive activity, is a sedentary and somewhat lonely occupation. If very able individuals are far removed from the average, then they will necessarily tend to be solitary for lack of congenial companions. The results on the Eysenck, therefore, came as something of a surprise. With the exception of two girls, the remaining eleven scored above the average norms for their age on the extraversion scale. This may have been a function of the group's stage of development, since Junior children could be normally expected to be gregarious and outgoing. The brightest boy had the highest score for extraversion, and the brightest girl the next. Yet when speaking individually to the group, and to these two in particular, the initial impression received was one of shyness and reticence. The boy, in fact, had developed a façade for social use with adults, which a deeper acquaintance proved to be a pose. At first, there was a decided playing-down of his abilities and interests, and an apparent lack of enthusiasm for conversation. His preferred role was that of the buffoon and clown, and he seemed to be silly deliberately to counter possible criticism. When he relaxed, and felt himself free of critical observation, he emerged as one of the leaders of the group, who initiated and directed many of their work and play activities and discussions. This misleading first impression was noticeable with all these children although to a lesser degree. Their natural inclinations were those of the practical, gregarious, talkative extravert.

The group also all scored below average on the norms for their age on the Lie Scale, which is incorporated within the introversion-extraversion dimensions. Terman's original observation with regard to the personal characteristics of able children is worth recalling: namely, that, contrary to uninformed opinion, such children are morally dependable. A student also used a so-called Morality Test, which was adapted from Getzels and Jackson's [20] work with American 6th graders, and she also found their scores to be above average for reliability. These results should obviously be interpreted with caution, but they seem to invite further inquiry, preferably on a larger, and more varied population.

Highly intelligent children, it would appear, seem positively to enjoy an enigmatic role, until they feel understood, and can relax with people they know, and be the selves they truly are. From the practising teacher's point of view, this must present an annoying Jekyll and Hyde problem which needs time for resolution. Only at the end of the first term at the College did this group talk freely with adults on the level of maturity that was natural to them, and which they realized was acceptable. It is not considered that the College had any superior influence in this matter; but these children all suggested, directly as well as by inference, that they were unnecessarily "squashed" by adults generally, and this unpleasing attitude is not likely to endear them to their teachers. At the age of nine they did not view adults as being particularly omnipotent (possibly an adolescent characteristic and inevitable anyway), and quickly saw ridiculous elements in pompous situations. By way of illustration: one afternoon, when they had left me to do some earth science, they were studying worms (annelida) in the biology laboratory with an enthusiastic student. The latter naturally, and spontaneously, used the correct names for her specimens. A casual onlooker was fairly obviously out of her depth, and after attempts at conversation, patted the brightest boy on the head and said, "Isn't this fun! What do you call this worm, dear?" She was told that the worm was called "Fred." The boy was equally capable of replying that it was "a sanguineous annelid," but apparently thought that "Fred" was the appropriate answer for childish adults. He was quite polite, so the questioner was more puzzled than indignant. The incident is also typical of the hazards of disciplining such children: it is very difficult to be precise as to why such behaviour is unacceptable without becoming more involved in the pomposity that sparks it off. A sense of humour is then the teacher's saving grace.

A highly developed sense of the ridiculous was common to the whole group, and one of the stories they liked was written by the youngest girl (then only eight) during their first term at the College.

The Spanial (sic) *with no ears*

Once upon a time there was a spanial called Jingles. Now, when Jingles was a pup he had had a fight with a cat and strangely enough the cat had bitten off Jingles ears. As spanials usually have long ears, Jingles Mistress had tied on two sausages in the place of his ears, but every time he had some new sausages he bit them off and ate them. So in the end his mistress rolled two pieces of paper up and soaked them in tea and tied them on on Jingles. So that whenever he tried to bite them off he got a terrible taste.

Returning to the second personality test used—the M.B.T.I.— which is also based on Jungian typology, this measure was adopted in order to assess a subtler dimension than the more usual introversion-extraversion dichotomy, namely, intuition. Interested readers are referred to the Manual accompanying the test for detailed information concerning the intuitive type of personality, or the N index, as it is called therein. Briefly, according to the conceptual scheme on which the test is based, intuition is a form of perception, or an indirect way of becoming aware of people, things and ideas. Intuitive types are sensitive individuals with insight, or a good understanding of themselves, and also usually a good understanding of others. They are likely to be characterized by high intelligence. This generalization, in particular with reference to intelligence, does not enjoy uniform support, but it is a matter of both observation and experience that able children can be highly sensitive, empathic types. This "talent for feeling," as it was described by Jung [31], was thought important enough to merit investigation for two reasons. Intuitive individuals tend to become the victims of their own sensitivity, and shrink from making either themselves or their opinions effective, a form of behaviour which could be subversive to the gifts which these very able children hold in trust; and also, intuition is thought to relate to creativity (this latter aspect is discussed more fully elsewhere).

The group was given the questions which relate to the N index, and, as anticipated, their answers were in agreement with the answers which could be expected of intuitive types. For example, to the question, "Which word in this pair appeals to you most: (*a*) build, (*b*) invent?" they chose (*b*), which is one of the preferences subsumed under the N index.

Since there was some probability, albeit slender, that these children might also be divergent or creative thinkers, as well as obviously good at answering traditional I.Q. tests, it was decided to try the more open-ended kinds of activities suggested by the Minnesota Tests of Creative Thinking [21]. They were asked to complete and name ambiguous shapes; to incorporate circles in pictures, using as many ideas as they could think of; and to suggest ways of improving two toys—a teddy bear and a hedgehog. Attempts to score their efforts numerically proved so frustrating that it was decided to look for some of the main criteria of divergent thinking: originality (based on answers much less common than the usual stereotypes), wit, humour and phantasy, and elaboration of ideas.

Circles were incorporated into pictures depicting unusual eye-views of various objects: for example, the rear view of an elephant. When faces were drawn (which is normally the commonest response) they were elaborated by being given expressions, or nonsensical names, and one was just coloured red and left as a bulbous nose. The usual response to completing two little horn-shaped drawings is to turn them into pixies; none of these children chose the obvious stereotype, but gave such replies as "dancing fish," or drew "Hornwhiskers the Cow." Their strongest card was humour and phantasy—the verbal pun, the juxtaposition of unlikely ideas. Experienced teachers would probably agree that verbal wit is a typical, and sometimes irritating, characteristic of very intelligent pupils. In this instance it was positively encouraged, and caused prolonged fits of giggles, which were controllable in such a small group.

They were once asked what their favourite jokes happened to be at the time, and the following are two examples of their idea of the acme of wit—

A man went to America where he met an Indian who had a fantastic memory. The man asked the Indian what he had had for breakfast three years ago. The Indian replied, "Fish." A year later, the man went to the Indian and greeted him by saying, "How," and the Indian then replied, "Fried."

Once in a theatre there was a comedian and he was just running out of jokes when all the lights went off. Then a Chinese man came in and said, "Everybody that can't see, put up your hands." Everybody put up their hands and the lights came on. The comedian was amazed and he asked the Chinese man how he did it. The Chinese man said, "Many Hands Make Light Work."

The improvement of toys was largely functional: ways of causing them to move and talk were offered, to make them more interesting. Slots were inserted for pennies, to obtain orange drinks from one ear and chocolate from the legs. Excretory functions were also suggested, but this had been anticipated.

In sum, their ideas were non-stereotyped, and fluent, in that one suggestion quickly generated others, and this seemed to indicate, therefore, that one of the divergent thinking factors was present, defined by Guilford [24d] as "the ability to call up many ideas in a situation relatively free from restriction."

As will be seen, however, when discussing their activities in the next chapter, the expectations of creative work, viewed practically and externally, were not entirely realized.

8 *Activities and Conclusions*

Part I: PATRICIA MELDON,
B.Sc., M.A., Ph.D.

It is not intended to describe the activities of the children referred to in Chapter 7 in detail, firstly because, as already adumbrated, they were consciously biased towards general classroom practice, and secondly because the main burden of the systematic observation undertaken was to discover what was of relatively most significance to the group's development, and what were the aspects on which it might be most worth while for busy teachers to concentrate. Remembering that they were young Juniors, we began informally with what might be described as cognitive play. They were given constructional toys: science and engineering kits, bricks, and large coloured pieces of wooden apparatus (Bilofix), complete with spanners, nuts and bolts.

During the first term, we travelled every Friday afternoon to one of the three contributing schools, and all thirteen joined together in one tiny room. The atmosphere was purposely permissive, but we often had to spread on to the stairs and landing. So, although conditions may have been what some Primary Schools have come to accept as "normal," they were not exactly ideal.

The children were willing and able to carry on without supervision if required, but to my surprise seemed somewhat lacking in ideas. The girls were equally interested in the Meccano and other conventionally masculine toys, but they produced stereotyped houses mainly, while the boys made "exterminators," ray-guns, and "obliterators." They all appeared happier with the instruction booklets, and given this base they proved to be more inventive. They were also rather inept when it came to using tools:

open-ended spanners were constantly being dropped, and they applied the wrong alternative end to the wooden nuts, which caused cross-threading so that nuts and bolts were jammed. It is thought that ring spanners would have proved equally troublesome. In anticipation of later conclusions, they need precise teaching in techniques, and it is suggested that intellectually able children be given such expertise immediately. They are frustrated by lack of "know-how" because they have ideas which they cannot execute, yet find the business of using simple tools easy to understand. If learning such techniques is delayed, they are then bored and exasperated by having to stop and master them. Anticipating this requirement seems preferable to waiting until the need arises.

Their paintings, mosaic pictures, puppets, and work with natural materials, junk, and clay, were similarly unadventurous until they were given suggestions and the skills of working with their chosen media. This may have been a function of the non-specialism of their teacher; perhaps these activities are more productive in the hands of a teacher with the creative insights of the artist, and one used to working within the discipline of various media. Or perhaps they needed someone convinced of the value of allowing children to discover by experiment with a minimum of adult direction. Initially, with clay for example, they all produced animals with homely little faces—honest, unpretentious efforts—and, although I found them pleasing, it is probably correct to describe them as unadventurous.

We also tried percussive musical instruments, such as xylophones, dulcimers and chime bars, with which they experimented separately and as a group. We were experimenting with sound, and, since there was no attempt to teach notation, music existed for them only momentarily in time. For them to derive any satisfactory pleasure, therefore, it was found that simple time signatures were necessary teaching points. Their music was contained by giving them words and jingles for which they had to find tunes, and they preferred playing together, though it was noisier than having to go away singly and make up individual rhythms.

A more memorable activity was introduced by a capable student who happened to be interested in archaeology, and whose ideas coincided with the known propensity of most Juniors to be natural scavengers. One of the children was discussing a museum which had been started at his school. A parent had found a piece of pottery which was apparently of some age; a local museum had been able to date it; and it was presented to the school. This caused some discussion on how people might know the age of such findings, and where the piece might have come from originally. The group appeared to have a reasonable concept of time in this connection, because they were very scornful of a boy they knew who had brought in an old bicycle wheel for a pre-historic museum. They actually described it as "incongruous."

The student decided to give them some practical work, so he went to a local junk shop and bought a cracked china bowl— white, with pink rosebuds. He broke the bowl into large pieces and later on asked the group to try to reconstruct the original shape. They were given a special glue, and after more discussion, drew what they though it might have looked like, and talked more about what it could have been used for. One of the boys had picked a specially large, round piece, with one rosebud on it, and looked speculatively at us, but the unspoken question was quickly denied!

They puzzled over this for nearly an hour, and when they had reconstructed it, decided that it must be modern because of the china mark underneath, and that it was probably a fruit bowl which was never full, because the bottom half of the pattern was worn.

Attempts at creative activity led on to creative writing, and they were relatively most fluent with themes based on scientific fiction and phantasy. For example, they once decided to describe imaginary beasts, and the following extracts are typical—

". . . the Greech came from an antelope and elephant. Its colour is green with yellow adjustments. Its teeth are ferocious, and it swallows things up in gulps without chewing them, and leaves (sic) its prey to its 91 stomachs because it eats such big things. The 91st stomach is left for sorting out bones, stones, or rocks and other things it does not fancy. You may think that it would not eat things it does not like, but it has a little brain. It also carries around a little coal bunker for fuel. It came (sic) extinct because it could not remember not to shut its sharp teeth on its tongue which made it lose blood . . . ."

". . . a liboon is brown with orange stripes—it has a short fluffy tail. Its fur is very thin except its tail . . . a liboon is very long and fat in all directions. A liboon only eats wool and cotton, so you will often see liboons stealing your woolen (sic) jumpers and things made of cotton . . . a liboon snarls when he is eating his food and when he attacks other animals, when he walks he makes a constant grunting noise . . . a liboon lives in a very deep hole, and when he likes, he can change his hole . . . ."

". . . a new-born idiodo is about 6 yards long and is born covered with stripes (which have to be bitten off by the mother when the baby is 2 weeks old) . . . common idiodos are usually a very pale blue with a white underneath, but all the royal family are born scarlet and stay that colour all their lives . . . ."

". . . a solon comes from a planet in the fourth galaxy; it has a fiery atmosphere so a Solon has a fire-proof skin . . . ."

(This is reminiscent of a story about a hobbit-like animal who lived behind a fireplace and had to wear asbestos shoes when he crossed the hearth; but the creator of the Solon had never heard of him.)

". . . the cowpotimus has to breathe tear gas, so it lives in holes in the ground and lives on the plant Tear . . . the grown-ups sometimes eat the young girls . . . they have no memorys (sic)."

A television programme concerning the *Marie Celeste* had aroused their interest; the idea of a ghost ship is likely to have universal appeal at this age, but they wanted to follow it through and consider as many explanations as possible, because they insisted that there must be some rational cause. Stories about monsters of the deep inevitably included the legend of the Kraken, and their imaginations were stirred by thoughts of what such a creature must have been like. How could it have survived at such depths, without light, and at such pressures? Their knowledge of such matters was both factual and accurate. Some of them made Krakens, out of junk, chicken wire, natural materials, and plastic. As usual with their practical work, when given a choice of materials, they tended to use the lot rather than confine themselves to paper and crayon, and they produced bug-eyed, swivel-eyed, floppy creatures, spidery blobs, some faceless, some with mouths filled with fangs. They subsequently brought along books about the sea, and one boy found Tennyson's original poem on the Kraken, and Wyndham's novel on the same theme.

Two other activities, similarly scientifically based, led on to quite advanced discussion, and possible creative work. One idea was, in fact, suggested by a theme given to graduate engineers as a test of creativity. The children were asked to imagine a fictitious planet called Arcturus, whose inhabitants were bird-like creatures with claws for feet and three eyes, one of which was X-ray. Other conditions could have been imposed: Arcturus could have been a planet without oxygen. These creatures, however, had a low sales resistance, and the group had to describe them, and design tools and appliances which would be suitable.

All the houses suggested had perches; one thoughtful little girl designed slippers for the Arcturians to wear indoors, so that their sharp claws would not dig into the floor. Generally, however, the responses were aggressive ones: retractable claws for tearing prey in order to eat, appliances for breathing fire and toasting their enemies.

On the use of eyes, it was decided that the X-ray eye would be useful for watching television after being sent to bed, for reading into people's minds, or to examine whether or not a worm was carrying eggs—in which case it could be used to breed more worms rather than as an immediate meal. The idea of three eyes involved staff and students in an unforeseen discussion of binocular and monocular vision, and found one member of the staff, at least, somewhat at a disadvantage.

These children undoubtedly like factual information—knowledge for its own sake—and their response to informal activities is largely on an intellectual plane. On a second occasion, we brought along an inflatable globe, and asked them to choose a country. The activity we had in mind would have been stultified without the group's ready general knowledge and information, because we placed a wire outline over the continent they picked—which happened to be South America—and then twisted the outline out of shape. We then asked what they thought would happen if South America actually did change its shape as the wire had done. They considered the new mountains which might result, tidal waves, changed climatic conditions, and the effects on the inhabitants of the globe. This might have been impossible with less able Junior children, whose actual knowledge, ability to abstract, and concepts of space were less mature.

Such intellectual maturity, for this group anyway, was most apparent when expressed orally. Indeed, the whole group preferred discussion, and this desire was expressed in such statements as, "I like giving ideas, but not writing down," and "I like it better when we discuss something and not write." Some of their discussions and debates were taped, and then subjected to further discussion, and they mostly chose their own subjects. We showed them some pictures of modern art, and they were surprisingly conservative in their judgments. So they elected to talk about the abstractions of beauty and ugliness. One boy's concept of ugliness was his teacher, and of beauty, his five girl-friends. Another saw beauty in a rubbish dump because it had many "oddities"; another found harmony and order in a transistor circuit.

The notion that they can manage on their own seems to be a fallacious one. This attribute no doubt comes—with maturity, or *faute de mieux*—but they need specific skills in the use of books, and an understanding of what it means to complete a sustained piece of work. Since they have powers of concentration beyond their age, it would seem profitable to keep them deliberately going past the point where experience would dictate otherwise for the less able. When they think something is finished, they seem to close their minds; they have done their "stint." As it is, they receive a great deal of practice within "closed" systems of thought, and are given activities which their high powers of reasoning enable them to do very quickly. They are given problems where all the information necessary for their solution is present, and only interpolation is required. "Open" systems of thought, and more adventurous thinking, they are not so used to, where there are many possible answers or termini. They require adults, therefore, who can themselves tolerate ambiguity, rather than those who feel safe if there seems to be only one answer, and who will accept only that from a class.

They also need knowledgeable adults, particularly at the Primary stage, when a child's range of interests may be at a peak. Able children, in fact, would seem to require more teaching, not less: facts, ideas, suggestions, encouragement, within an atmosphere of disciplined but permissive orderliness. Teachers cannot be passive agents, but must actively teach; and group work seems to be the most logical approach within the more formal class techniques which in reality must still obtain.

They were not truly capable of genuine argument, in the sense that they could readily see the other person's point of view; but specific help seems to be indicated here, because they do have some empathic understanding in advance of their years. When they discussed discipline, for example, several were aware of the difficult-ties from a teacher's point of view—large numbers, tiring job—and one boy suggested that some teachers might be harsh because they were afraid of the class. They talked on, leaving their hearers rather disconcerted.

They appeared to be compulsive talkers. If they could not talk to each other then they talked to themselves, and one would be faced with collective monologues, accompanied by restless, aimless movements. This desire to talk, on their part, seems to be a con-scious need. As one boy remarked, in another context, with all the assurance of ten summers, "If my teacher would let me discuss more, I could contribute appreciably to the lesson." Moreover, since their wit is peculiarly verbal, it is better canalized into legal activities than employed in repartee with some unsuspecting adult. Indeed, unless one knows these children very well, attempts at facetiousness reap the whirlwind.

There are other needs, which are perhaps more debatable.

Part II: JEAN BRIGGS, M.A., A.K.C.

In September, 1967, gifted children were introduced for the first time to work with the closed-circuit-television system at Brentwood. The installation consisted of remote-control as well as manual cameras, and a video-tape recorder. It was hoped that not only would the children work with the equipment, but that having two camera chains it would be possible to collect on tape evidence of the way in which they set about the work. Two groups of children were involved, one selected for high I.Q. referred to in Chapter 2, the other, referred to in Chapter 6, for high rating in creativity tests. One group consisted of 13 children, the other of 15 children, aged 10–11, and they came to the studio on alternate weeks.

The purpose of the experiment was to see if the children could adapt their imaginative ideas to the discipline of the medium, and to observe the differences shown by the two groups. This was essentially a pilot project to consider the possible value of exposing the children to this type of creative experience, and to investigate ways in which this might best be done. Clearly, after only two terms' work, no definite conclusions can be made; the following points are merely observations.

Both groups of children were first introduced to the equipment and virtually allowed to play with it, so that they could get the feel of handling it, and at the same time work off their excitement at seeing one another on a television screen. Each child was given the opportunity to use both a remote-control and a manual camera, although it was intended that when they worked on their own programmes they should use only remote-control cameras, since the manuals were too heavy and too large for them to handle without adult help. They were also shown sound, lighting and recording equipment, but they were much too interested in the cameras ever to give much attention to any other studio equipment.

Our remote-control cameras are of an early industrial type which are difficult to handle well, in that they pan very slowly and over-shoot when panning has stopped. It was remarkable how rapidly some of the children in both groups learned not only to handle these cameras, but to compensate for the mechanical weaknesses. Four children, three boys from the creativity group and one girl from the I.Q. group, achieved this skill more quickly than any student or staff cameraman I have worked with. All the children, with the exception of one girl in the I.Q. group, enjoyed using the cameras—in fact, clamoured to use them to such an extent that meticulous rotas had to be observed. This interest was sustained. Some of the children, both boys and girls, never progressed beyond the stage of merely moving the cameras. Others, in varying degrees, not only developed technical skill but showed a sense of picture balance, of angles, of lighting effects. On the whole, the creativity group had the better camera sense.

No definite plan of work had been arranged. We hoped this would arise naturally from the children's reactions to the equipment. Because of the pattern imposed by camera practice in the control room, the children in both groups tended to form themselves into units of two or three. It was in these same "camera units" or "production crews" that they began to talk about suitable material for presenting on television. Students were available to help the children, but the ideas on content and presentation came entirely from the children themselves. In some groups there was argument about the subject to be chosen. In no instance, however, did the children try to form new groups with others who shared their interests; they remained strictly within their camera-units.

Our attention to equipment first, programme content second (which is reflected in this grouping) could well be criticized. It is certainly not an approach that could be justified in other circumstances, since it distorts the character of educational television. But in this instance it seemed that if the children were asked to consider subject-matter before they had some knowledge of the equipment, they would (a) think of their talks and plays in a classroom context and (b) need considerable guidance in selection— something which we particularly wished to avoid. As it was, all groups except one were aware of the need for visual interest in the form of illustrations or physical objects. This was important, since nearly all the children wanted to make information programmes on specialized subjects. Those of the high-I.Q. group included horses (two programmes), tortoises, Guiding. An interesting variation was produced by three boys who appeared as selectors for the next World Cup Series—informed discussion combined with drama. The creative group chose reptiles, stamps, coins and cars. Surprisingly, only one unit wanted to attempt creative drama.

Although the information programmes appear similar in character, there were certain interesting differences in the way in which the two groups tackled their material. The I.Q. group appeared to enjoy very much their sessions in the College library, reading, making notes and tracking down illustrations. They spent considerable time at home writing and re-writing their scripts, which in some cases were then typed. They were inclined, even within their units, to work very much in isolation, so that the result was often three separate talks on the same theme. Their illustrative material tended to come from books.

The children of the creativity group, on the other hand, tended to argue and discuss their way through to a final script which appeared in pencil on various scraps of paper. Their material tended to develop not from careful research but from what they had done or remembered themselves.

The children of the I.Q. group were not particularly interested in the programmes of other units in their group. They were reluctant to act as floor manager or caption operator when another pair of hands was needed. The creativity group was more co-operative. The play, for example, required a cast of many more than the two girls who wrote and produced it. Other children helped willingly, bringing their own clothes and props. They watched one another at work and offered advice (not always well received).

As the work progressed, a division began to appear in both groups between those who were more interested in presenting their programmes, and those who preferred working in the control room. There were boys and girls in both. One boy in the creativity group whose production ability was startling (that is, in the direction of cameramen and the selection of pictures) was hopelessly inadequate as a programme presenter, exhibiting the very faults on shot that, as a producer, he most severely attacked in others. (One of our most interesting pieces of tape shows his comments to his actors after an unsatisfactory rehearsal.) Two girls of the I.Q. group, who presented a charming little conversation on Guiding, were clumsy and unimaginative when handling cameras. Other children of the I.Q. group who, like them, were painstaking in their programme research and scripting, were unhappy with the necessarily impromptu nature of much camera work. These were encouraged to make simple camera scripts. The problem then was that those presenting the programme were not willing to go over their material again and again while the camera operators struggled for the perfection they seemed to want.

The most successful camera work was done by three boys in the creativity group, who from the start worked as a team. They allocated among themselves the roles of producer, number one cameraman and number two cameraman and worked at learning the techniques of their particular task. In the other units, the children tended to take turns at each job or argued as to who should produce. When there was no natural leader in the unit, this problem was never resolved. The leader of the three boys was, incidentally, the boy whose production ability has already been mentioned. His two cameramen also showed an amazing grasp of the essentials of visual presentation. A recording, made in the control room while they were working, indicates their confidence and awareness of the medium as well as the precision of their team work. Their conversation, while working, is an interesting blend of television jargon (which they were most anxious to learn and use) and schoolboy expression.

One girl in the I.Q. group also did some very promising work in production, although her method of achieving this was quite different. She used her cameramen not as a team but as puppets. She considered very carefully in advance how she wanted the cameras used, and then carried this out by means of very clear, quiet, detailed instructions.

The groups, however, have been too large to achieve as much as one might have hoped in the time. At the beginning of the course, when the children were occupied in preparing and writing their programmes, they could be continuously at work during the time that they were not taking part in rehearsals or acting as camera crew. Later, however, when the programmes were completed and the rehearsals for each item required longer time, there was a considerable amount of waiting about. Absence of students at this stage, on teaching practice, meant that no one was available to supervise work elsewhere. I had hoped that during recording some of the children would want to supervise lighting or sound or settings, but they were quite indifferent to what to them were very minor matters of production.

Another problem during this pilot experiment has been the fact that the children came to the studio only once a fortnight. This kind of creative work cannot be divided into sections which will be completed within a single afternoon. Too much time had to be spent in re-learning tricks of technique that had lost their edge in two weeks without practice. This meant, then, that progress was not rapid enough, and some of the children tired of the project. To sustain an imaginative stimulus and the tension which creative work requires, in these circumstances, is almost impossible.

Some of the children most interested in the work in closed-circuit television were dissatisfied when they saw the recordings of their own programmes. One of the most imaginative boys wished to re-make his. He could not, in fact, have improved on the programme without skilled adult direction. This raises the question of how far we should help the children in this sort of creative work. During this pilot year, we have encouraged the children to explore the medium with as little guidance as possible. The advantage of this has been that it has allowed us to see the way in which gifted children tackle a new challenge and a new discipline. Unfortunately, from the children's point of view, the end result does not have the quality which they imagine it ought to have, comparing it, as they inevitably do, with professional television programmes. It may be that in not giving more direction —that is, in not using trained expertise to achieve the technical effects which the children want—we are depriving them of taking part in programmes which would act both as a stimulus and as an example for future creative work.

It might be more effective, particularly in dealing with younger children, first to direct them in making a programme, using all the resources of the system, before inviting them to work on their own.

9 *Mathematics*

DOUGLAS COLLINS, B.Sc.

THIS chapter describes the experimental work done in mathematics with twelve children over a period of three years. In a short chapter it is not possible to cover in detail all the work done with these children, but an attempt has been made to describe the attitudes adopted, some of the experimental approaches used, the type of content material and some of the lessons learned from the work.

Two members of staff and several students were available to plan the work for this particular group of children. By chance one member of staff was a mathematician and the other was an artist. These members of staff and the students met to discuss the project and to prepare flexible plans of approach. The original idea was to devote half an afternoon session to Art and the other half to Mathematics, but during the discussions the idea of merging the two subjects was mentioned, and it was decided that, whilst integration of subjects was not the primary aim, there was a lot to be said for leaving the whole afternoon flexible in that Mathematics could be demanding the attention of some of the children while the others might be engaged in an Art activity. It was agreed that, wherever possible and desirable, a connection between the two subjects would be explored, and at other times the two subjects might drift apart. This arrangement was thought to be useful in that children, engrossed in one activity, be it Art or Mathematics, could continue after the afternoon break. It seemed reasonable to avoid stopping children from working on a topic just when their interest had been aroused.

The next question to be settled was, how should we go about the work? Should we "teach" them or should we avoid the ordinary classroom situation altogether? Once again the accent was on flexibility; sometimes we would use one approach and at other times different ones could be tried. By a similar process of discussion and argument we finally agreed that no form of class notebook would be used. It was felt that the children must record their work in the way *they* wanted. Our job would be to make certain the appropriate materials were available at the time.

At the start of the first lesson in Mathematics the children were encouraged to talk freely about their ideas concerning the subject. It seemed that all the children regarded the subject as being "full of sums." Some said it was "a bit boring, but very easy." Eventually, the lesson proper started. The subject was Binary Numbers, and the approach used here was quite simply the introduction of *a game*, the children being given a set of rules:—"Two items in a column are worth one in the column immediately to the left and vice-versa". The apparatus for playing such a game was suggested by the children themselves. Among the suggestions were—

   (i) Squared paper with 1's written in the columns.
  (ii) Plywood boards with columns of holes just large enough to take matchsticks.
 (iii) Rings on columns of pegs.
 (iv) Columns of tiddlywinks.
  (v) Rows of empty milk bottles.
 (vi) Teams of children in the playground.

We decided that each child could play the game as he wanted, excluding (vi) which would rob the others of the free choice. The problem of recording the result soon cropped up. One suggestion was "an X where there was an item and a 0 where there were empty columns." The idea of 1 for an item left over and a 0 to indicate an empty column came from the boy who was using matchsticks. His 1 was, in fact, just a drawing of a matchstick. Squared paper was made available and the children soon turned from the practical approach to a symbolic one. They quickly discovered that each number of objects started with, yielded its own pattern, which was then recorded thus—

0	0
1	1
2	10
3	11
4	100

It is interesting to note that no child called 10 "ten," as the symbols apparently meant something quite different from numbers. However, the question was posed, "could we add two of these 'patterns'?" I really expected the response, "who ever heard of adding patterns!" But no, the answer was, almost immediately, "we just put the two patterns together and continue playing the game." This was done several times, and after a while the fact was noticed that the resulting pattern went against the number which one would get when adding the appropriate numbers. Two girls were found actually doing the problems this way, not by playing the game, and getting their binary number by playing the game with the resultant number. There was no intention to cheat here—"It just seemed the obvious way." Before long, it seemed natural to speak of binary numbers and binary arithmetic, and over a period of about two weeks we returned often to this game, just for pleasure. When the problem of subtraction arose one day, the response from one girl was to take a pile of matches and to perform the subtraction using a decomposition method, that is, she played the game backwards where necessary, replacing one match in a column by two matches in the column to the right.

During the second half of this session the children were asked to examine a certain plant (spurge) for structure. The reply was that the plant tended to grow like railway lines, that is, one stem divided into two stems, each of which split again into two. The children were then asked whether they knew of another such plant or animal which exhibited this form in any way, but there was no response to this question. Bacteria were mentioned in the hope that some of the children had already come across their mode of reproduction. This, too, was outside their experience. However, when they were told of the way in which bacteria reproduce (one bacterium dividing to form two bacteria), they were so interested that the next ten minutes or so were given over to talking generally about bacteria and the ways in which they could harm man or benefit man. In following Art sessions, the children were asked to develop the binary form as an art form. This is described in Chapter 10.

The ability of these children to retain information and to put it to use later on is illustrated by the following account of what happened during another lesson six months later, when the children had been working with even numbers, odd numbers, and problems relating to continuous paths, such as the Konigsberg bridge problem and the problem of whether it was possible to draw a certain shape with a continuous sweep of the pencil. At the end of the session, the following question was asked: "What do you get if you add an odd number to an odd number?" One girl replied, "An even number" straight away. When asked how she had obtained that answer, she said, "An odd number written in binary form always has a 1 in the first place. When two such numbers are added, the two 1's combine to give a 0 in the first place with 1 to carry, and a binary number with a 0 in the first place is an even number." Of course, an answer in this form was not expected. This girl was nine years old at the time.

The work done so far indicated that the interest of the children was easily aroused by the type of work which they found unusual, especially if the work was presented either as a puzzle or as a game of some sort. They were not at all interested in work they had already mastered and which was not being developed. Sums, as such, were considered boring and useless. One boy said, "If I wanted to work it out I could, but why should I bother when the answers are not interesting?" It soon becomes clear that gifted children are not encouraged in any way by merely increasing the number, or even the difficulty, of ordinary problems. This approach can do nothing but harm. After all, one of the primary aims in any work attempted must be to evoke interest and enthusiasm.

The question arose one afternoon during discussions with students as to whether these children would pursue a difficult problem if they were interested in the approach but not particularly interested in the problem itself, that is, would they rise to a challenge and stick to it until they broke through? It was pointed out by one student that, in the work done so far, the children had met with nothing but success, and, whilst it was clear that success inspired more success, it would be interesting to see how they would behave when faced with a difficult situation, preferably an unexpected one. We decided to put them to the test. The topic chosen was "sets." In the first lesson, the idea of a set was established in a general way. We had previously decided not to take up the time of the pupils with matters of notation, so words like "intersection," "union" and the like were not used. The children were encouraged to explain matters in their own words and with the help of a diagram (Venn diagram) when one was needed. It was quite noticeable that the students taking the lessons soon picked up the vocabulary used by the children to describe their work, and terms such as "the overlap," "the whole lot," "the red bit," and so on, were used quite freely. On the whole, the work proceeded quite satisfactorily along these lines and the children were displaying interest. When the next week's lesson came along, the children were given one or two easy problems involving two sets and one quite difficult problem involving three sets (this problem had been taken from last year's C.S.E. paper, and the C.S.E. candidates had been expected to use an algebraic symbol, x, to represent the number of elements in one section of a Venn diagram and then to work on from there). We decided to give the question in its raw state without hints on approach. We agreed that the children would probably meet with failure, and that the realization of failure was what we were out to observe, together with the children's subsequent actions. The questions had been written on the blackboard before the start of the lesson, and the children were just given large sheets of paper and were told to work at the problems. The easy problems were soon out of the way and most children were at work on the hard problem. For ten minutes or so the room was quiet. Then the first child who thought he had a solution attracted the attention of the student taking the lesson. The student checked the solution by adding together the elements in the various parts of the diagram. Alas, the total was not correct and the pupil returned to his seat with a puzzled look on his face. This story was repeated for every member of the class. After a few more minutes they started to fidget. Then they started moaning aloud that there was something wrong with the question. Their next reaction was to compare their papers. One child went so far as to check the work of every other member of the class. Suddenly, it seemed that the whole group was in conference over the problem. Their concerted opinion was that the question was wrong in some way, so the question was examined step-by-step. Nothing suspicious could be found, a few more minutes passed, and the children were seen to be doodling, with no apparent effort being made to solve the problem. They had lost interest in it. Or had they? After a while, one girl said quietly, "I think I've got it all to fit." On examination, her solution was found to be correct, and she was congratulated. The revival of activity was remarkable. When she returned to her seat, her work was examined by the other pupils, one after the other. Their approach now seemed to be to take just one section of the correct answer and to use it as a starting point for their own work. Needless to say, correct solutions came flowing in. We were very surprised to find that the children were just as pleased as if they had managed to solve the problem without difficulty. The girl who had started the chain reaction received no credit from them for her help, indeed, it was noticeable that the most extroverted of the boys was busily explaining to her how the problem should have been tackled. This lesson, and several like it, indicated that the minds of able children work on, even when they give no sign of application to the problem. Less able children, when appearing to have given up a problem, have usually stopped working on it altogether, and seldom return to it. The question is, to what extent can gifted children be allowed to doodle in the ordinary classroom? Whilst it is true that their minds may still be hard at work, it is difficult to tell. On the other hand, should we always expect outward signs that a mind is hard at work? One thing we could agree on was this: these children, like all others, needed a steady succession of successes leading them towards the difficult work they were required to master. The chance of mastery seems to increase with each ounce of success. This would indicate the need for carefully graded work. If real difficulties are met with too soon, the more able children begin to look for reasons why they do not really want to know the answer to a problem, even after a period of persistence. The real difference between them and the less able lies in the duration of this persistence period. We were a little surprised to find that these gifted children were just as keen to get little meaningless rewards as all children. Red stars, team points, etc., were received with great pleasure, even when there were no teams. One boy put it into words: "I like marks—I'm very interested in getting marks." Pleasing the teacher is also a strong motivating force with them, in common with other children, but a careless rebuke can often penetrate more deeply than with other children. We found that great care was needed in the choice of words if any form of rebuke was to be given. Naturally, we should have preferred not to rebuke at all.

One of the lessons learned from this work is that these children still need a concrete introduction to a topic before they venture on to abstract ground. Students often offered the argument that since these children are highly intelligent it is quite in order to introduce new work in an abstract fashion. The children themselves had a contempt for practical work and were quite loth to continue a practical venture once they thought they had seen what the end-point would be. The fact that they were often wrong in their intuitive judgments made little difference to this attitude. In fact, if experience indicated a different result from that which they had anticipated, they would often ignore the experimental result and return to their original idea with their faith unshaken. On one occasion I was most disappointed to find that the children were actually falsifying the results of experiments to fit in with what they thought ought to happen. There are good grounds here for discussing with the children the philosophy behind the work, and this was done as often as time permitted. They were given accounts, from the history of the physical sciences, of instances where scientists had refused to accept the results of experiment if these results differed from their own theories. The children said that they thought this was a dreadful state of affairs, and asked how extremely clever people could do such a thing. Yet they were quite willing to do the same themselves, even after such discussions. To give an example, I recall the afternoon when the children were asked to predict the result when twenty coins were tossed fifty times. This followed a series of lessons and experiments in probability. The children had sufficient experience and knowledge to know that the results could not be predicted with any degree of accuracy. We hoped that they would pick a *likely* result and make the comment that it was quite possible for anything else to happen. Most of them picked results which had a high degree of likelihood, e.g., 450 heads and 550 tails, 467 heads and 533 tails, and they went away to find out what would happen if they actually tossed this number of coins the number of times stated. They were watched closely but unobtrusively by students, and over half the children recorded results very close to their predictions, although the actual results of their experiments were at variance with them. In the discussions which followed, none would admit this, and we came to the conclusion that there had been an element of competition present which had led to an overwhelming urge to get the "correct" answer, i.e., the one they had predicted. In the Art session which followed this activity, the children discussed "Fibs, fables and stories," the session providing a follow-up to what had gone before. Where the abstract work followed practical work, the practical work providing the grounds for further thought, this deviation from the "honest path" happened less frequently and the practical results were held in higher esteem. In addition to this, the children seemed more able to return to the practical work to check on some thought they might have had, or to solve a practical problem with the help of theoretical knowledge. One lesson was specifically designed to find out whether the children were able to put the results of theory into practice, and the following is an account of that experimental lesson.

The students, after discussion, prepared a lesson in geometry leading to the "Mid-point Theorem" (the line joining the mid-points of two sides of a triangle is parallel to and half the length of the remaining side). Incidentally, this violated the rule that we were not to anticipate Secondary-school work, but the students were so keen to put this lesson into operation that I had not the heart to stop them, especially as they hoped to prove a point. The lesson was given formally, that is, the usual notion of congruence was developed and the properties of straight lines and angles revised. The children proved to have a good background knowledge of these topics already. However, each fact needed for the main part of the lesson was recorded carefully on the blackboard and the children were tested orally on these facts to make sure that they understood them. The students then proceeded to enunciate and prove the theorem. It seemed that the children were encountering no difficulties; indeed, they thought that it was all "pretty obvious". To test their understanding further, the students gave them a simple rider which was solved quickly. This was taken as proof that the aim of the lesson had been achieved, namely, to get the children to understand the theorem and its proof. One of the two students, who had been briefed separately before the lesson, then gave out to the class scissors, plain paper and large gummed triangles cut from coloured paper. The children were given these instructions—

(i) Take the triangle and cut it so that the pieces will reassemble to form a parallelogram.

(ii) Stick the pieces onto the plain paper to show the parallelogram, and draw a diagram, or two, to show how it was done.

The fact that no part of the triangle was to be wasted was stressed. It proved disappointing to the students in that not one child succeeded in carrying out the task allotted. After all, the given triangle had only to be cut along a line joining the mid points of two sides, and the small triangle cut off to be moved round to one end, where it could be arranged to give the required parallelogram. The diagram from the earlier part of the lesson was still on the blackboard. Even though plenty of spare triangles had been made available for use if mistakes were made in the initial cut, the children were curiously hesitant in making that first cut; they hated making mistakes, and this was the factor which seemed to hold them back. Much encouragement was needed to make them experiment with the triangles, and one boy even came along with tears in his eyes and a handful of mutilated triangles to confess that he "had made a mess of it." He appeared surprised when we said that it did not matter and that there were plenty of spare triangles for him to work on. Could it be, we wondered, that the "war against waste" is responsible for this attitude? However, more to the point, it was quite clear that these children did not relate the practical work to the work which had preceded it on the blackboard. When the connection was pointed out to them, they exclaimed "of course!"

The students said that they had found this experiment interesting, even though the practical work introduced at the end was "a dirty trick." The children asked why they had not done the practical work first. "Out of the mouths of babes and sucklings . . ." The following lesson was given over to practical work of this nature but with no formal geometry to follow. Among the tasks they were asked to do were the following—

  (i) From a triangle make a parallelogram (now found easy).

  (ii) From a parallelogram make a rectangle.

  (iii) From a triangle make a rectangle.

  (iv) From a square make a pentagon with three equal sides.

  (v) From a rectangle make a kite.

Once again they were supplied with gummed coloured paper cut to form the starting shapes. One girl asked if she could do the problems by drawing. "I hate messing about with all this stuff," she said. I suspect that some of the other children agreed with her. This was yet another example of their distaste for practical work. More reference to this attitude will be found in Chapter 10.

After a slow start they fairly romped along; the snipping of their scissors made short work of each problem in turn. They even spotted the trick problem (deliberately inserted) where the task could not be completed without reversing the paper, which meant that the gum was on the wrong side. This problem they solved by cutting two equal shapes, one the mirror image of the other, and forming two end products. An example of this is found in the task of forming a kite from a rectangle.

One interesting fact emerged from this work. It was that the students found the tasks difficult whereas the children now found them easy. I hasten to add that this is in no way a reflection on the students; it is just that they had fierce competition from very able children.

I would argue, from our work along these lines, that the formal geometry is best left until later but that much geometry can be done by using a practical approach to problems in mathematics. It is also possible to find much geometry in Art and Craft, and this source of geometrical beauty should never be left idle. It is true that this work will not enable children to quote theorems and to write out formal proofs, and their knowledge is not in the form where it can be tested formally, but I suggest that knowledge is "still there" in the form of assimilated experience which, I venture to add, will make their future work more enjoyable and more understandable. In this type of practical work the more able child can still work at a level which provides a challenge to his intellect, and he can far outstrip his less able classmates. If a child has the ability to experiment, he should be given ample opportunity to exercise that ability. Sometimes a great deal of encouragement will be needed because of this tendency to avoid practical work.

Another advantage which able children have over the less able is that they often see *reasons* why a certain procedure is successful. They are not content with knowing that a certain procedure *works*, they want to know how and why it works. This was demonstrated one afternoon when one of the boys brought with him a set of numbers written in columns on a card. The game was this: first a person acting as a subject was asked to select a number from the card but not to divulge the number. Then the subject was asked to answer yes or no when asked whether this number appeared in each of the columns. At the end of this questioning, the subject was told which number he had chosen. This game amused and interested these children intensely. They wanted to know *how* the game worked. Now, an activity had already been planned for that afternoon and two students were prepared with apparatus and lesson notes to conduct this activity. However, after a very hurried consultation, we decided to see how far we could utilize this pre-formed interest, and before I describe the activity that followed, perhaps I ought briefly to explain the "game" which the boy had brought along. This is the card—

16	8	4	2	1
17	9	6	3	3
18	10	5	6	5
19	11	7	7	7
20	12	12	10	9
21	13	13	11	11
22	14	14	14	13
23	15	15	15	15
24	24	20	18	17
25	25	21	19	19
26	26	22	22	21
27	27	23	23	23
28	28	28	26	25
29	29	29	27	27
30	30	30	30	29
31	31	31	31	31

Suppose a subject chooses the number 27. Let 1 denote that 27 is present in a particular column and 0 denote that it is absent from a column. When he gives his answers (yes or no) they will be, corresponding to the column order:

	yes	yes	no	yes	yes
or in terms of 1 and 0	1	1	0	1	1

Now 11011 is the binary representation of 27, and the person who receives these answers can work out the number selected by the subject. In fact, he is saved this trouble by having at his disposal, written as the first number in each column, the value of a 1 in that column. For example, a 1 in the centre column has value 4, and this is the first number in the column. We see that when the answer "yes" is given the number at the head of that column is added to the running total, and when the answer "no" is given the corresponding number is ignored. Returning to the number 27 for a moment, we see that the following numbers are added—

	16	8	4	2	1
	yes	yes	no	yes	yes
	add 16	add 8	ignore	add 2	take 1
Running total	27	11	3	3	1

It was clear that all the children present knew how to work the game, so there was no opportunity to get them to discover this. It was also clear that not one of them realised *how* it worked. The children were given a large sheet of paper each, and they were asked to construct a similar game, but using different numbers at the head of each column. For example, the numbers might be—

25	12	9	7	3

They all did this with comparative ease, and two points emerged. It was found that—

(i) Not all the numbers in the range chosen could be incorporated in the columns, for example, in the list above the numbers 1, 2, 4, 6 (among others) would not appear.

(ii) Sometimes a number could be incorporated in different ways, for example, using the list above, 19 could go in columns headed by 12 and 7 or in columns headed by 3, 7 and 9.

Despite these difficulties, the children first found that their games worked, and they knew *why* they worked since they had constructed their games to a certain pattern. The next task was to try to get the children to concentrate on removing the two difficulties encountered earlier. They were asked to tackle the first problem, that is, how to close the gaps. One point emerged immediately, that is, the first column must be headed by a 1. They were then left to ponder over this problem. Within seconds they were working in groups of about three, and one or two heated discussions were taking place. Suddenly, they hit on the solution. Their argument was quite logical: "You must have a 1, otherwise 1 will not appear at all. You must have a 2, otherwise 3 cannot be included. Since 3 can be formed from 2 and 1 by addition, 3 appears in the column headed by 2 and in the column headed by 1, it need not head a column itself . . . ." They noted that the second difficulty had also been overcome. One of the students then tried to get them to appreciate the binary nature of the game, but even after several leading questions they were unable to do this. Finally, the children ventured to suggest that the answers yes-no could be given as 1/0, but they did not relate this to the game until a specimen game was played with the answers 1/0 being written on the blackboard to form a binary number. At this point, the structure of the game became clear to them.

During the discussion which followed this lesson, the students agreed that the teacher in the classroom would find it difficult to give the amount of attention needed for an activity of this kind, that is, an activity devised at short notice to exploit the interest of one or two clever children. There would be the rest of the class to consider. The question was posed, would it be possible to conduct a modified version of this lesson with less able children and to achieve roughly the same results? It was felt that this might be possible and the students took a note to this effect. However, when an opportunity arose a few months later, and this activity was tried with less able children of the same age, the students met with complete failure. Only one pupil in the class was able to construct a game which would work, and no pupil got further than the stage of trying to write his own card of numbers. The students pointed out that the motivation present with the able children, that is, the fact that *they* had produced the card and had asked how it worked, was not present with the less able children who had the game thrust upon them. The general conclusion reached was that it would be difficult, and wrong, to take the interests of two or three of the more able children in a class and to devise from them activities for the whole class. The interests of *any* pupil might provide useful activity work at more than one level, the more able being allowed, or encouraged, to take a topic further. The greatest difficulty here seems to be concerned with maintaining continuity of subject matter. Working from the chance interests of children can result in isolated topics being studied with no thought of progression. I feel that teachers of mathematics will agree that when motivation is seen to be strong, the resulting work is worth while, even if isolated, in that it imparts a fresh flavour to the subject. Often the teacher will be able to link up with other work, and this is more to the good.

In this chapter I have concentrated so far on the purely mathematical work that was done with these children. I want now to give an illustration of the type of work which lent itself particularly well to Mathematics and to Art. Indeed, in one topic (tessellations) the best work was done under the heading of Art. The children were asked on one occasion, when investigating the properties of shapes, in a series of lessons on symmetry, to find out which shapes would fit together leaving no spaces. They encountered no difficulties with this work until they were asked to devise shapes of their own which would tessellate. The results were not very encouraging until it was pointed out to them that if one started with one shape which would tessellate, then certain modifications to the shape, provided each shape was treated equally, would result in a new shape which would still tessellate. An interesting lesson followed, where the children were given squared paper or triangulated paper, and were asked to produce tessellations. Several good pieces of work resulted from this. Then the children were asked if they could produce a shape which tessellated in *more than one direction* and they were shown one example (see Fig. 1.). Half an hour of hard work yielded little, so they were shown more examples and were allowed to study these examples closely. Even so, no results were forthcoming. At this point we decided to tackle this topic from another viewpoint, and the work was taken over into the Art sessions, when the children studied tiles. The interest aroused was

Fig. 1.

truly remarkable and the progress made was most encouraging. This work is fully described in Chapter 10.

As already mentioned, the underlying attitude adopted towards the work done with this set of children was one of experiment. Whilst the classroom situation has its advantages, we felt that here was an opportunity to experiment with different lines of approach. Some of the approaches used might ordinarily be considered bad teaching practice, but in the conditions we were enjoying, even bad methods were worth trying. Here is an account of how a bad teaching method actually blossomed into something worth while.

On one afternoon, the room in use was cleared of all objects and materials save for chairs, tables, calculating machines, paper and large charts of ordinary sums of all types. On arrival, the children were told that they could do anything they wanted (within reason) except that they must stay in the room. After a short while they were asking questions about the calculating machines (they had not used such machines before) but we refused to answer their questions in detail and they were told to find the answers for themselves.

After half an hour, one child had discovered how to make a machine add numbers and had succeeded in finding the correct answer to one of the displayed problems. The other children clustered round her and watched her repeat the procedure, after which they tried the process out on a machine of their own. Not long afterwards the processes, in outline, of subtraction and multiplication were discovered and more problems were solved.

At this point we decided to start answering their questions. They wanted to know what "this little knob does" and how three numbers could be multiplied together. The method of instruction used was to gather the children together, away from the machines, and to demonstrate a single procedure (the back-transfer, for instance) and then to send them back to their machines to try it out. It was generally agreed that they had learnt a great deal in a short time, but one of the students asked whether they would have learnt even faster if a traditional method of instruction had been used. We decided to put this to the test with another class. The method adopted here was to give each child a machine, and attempt to teach the routines step by step. This lesson was a complete failure. Firstly, the children fiddled with the machines during the explanations, with the consequence that many machines were jammed before any procedure had been attempted. Secondly, some of the children missed some of the explanation at each stage because they had been busy asking the pupil next door whether this or that was the right lever. This meant that explanations had to be repeated often. The amount of work covered turned out to be minimal. These experiments and several which followed indicated that the able children are quite capable of working in twos or threes with a calculating machine without any initial instruction. Active teaching in this field seems to do most good when the children ask for it. Even so, it is often only necessary to teach one child and then allow the information to spread. The less able children do respond a little to the same approach, but their interest seems to wane at the same point where the interest of the able children bursts forth. There is much to be said for having a "machine bay" where children can be sent in pairs to learn to use a calculating machine.

One of the most refreshing qualities about this particular group of children was their ability to laugh at their own mistakes and then to improve their technique. An example of this was seen when the children were sent out to measure the height of a building using the "shadow method." During a brief chat it was discovered that the children possessed an intuitive idea of proportion, and it was decided to put their ideas to use. Each child was given a stick, about twenty inches long, and a yard rule. The group was then told to use these pieces of apparatus to find the height of a building. They proved quite capable of doing this and the arithmetic proved to be no barrier. However, three of the children were late in returning to the classroom. When asked what had kept them, they blushed and said that they had positioned the stick in the ground and had carefully measured its length, but when they had come to measure the length of the shadow, they found that the sun was no longer shining and had to wait for it to reappear. "What we should have done was to measure the shadow first, because the length of the stick could be measured whether the sun was shining or not," they said, looking past me at the rest of the children, who were enjoying the joke. Ten minutes later, when the results of their measurements had been displayed on a blackboard in histogram form and the children were asked for comments, they said "Surely you didn't expect all the answers to be the same?" This remark appeared to remove the need for talking about "personal errors" and the like.

To conclude this chapter I would remark that the atmosphere created by this group of children was most certainly due to the fact that adults were "interested" in the work they were doing. Often, adults would enter the room and work with the children at the same task and would not hesitate to ask the children for advice or to admit that the children were better than they were at a particular activity. In consequence, the children were at one and the same time confident and modest; they could adjust themselves instantly to the person talking to them. The most pleasing remark passed by one of the children was in answer to a question put to them by a visitor. The visitor asked, "Don't you think it's a waste of time travelling here to do your work?" The child replied, "Travelling is always a waste of time, but we make up for it when we get here."

10 *Art with Mathematics*

ROBERTA G. EVERETT, A.T.D.

WHEN the experiment which Mr. Collins has just described was being considered, work on the project in the College had been going on for about a year. Nevertheless, there was complete freedom of thought. During our discussions on planning, however, it was suggested that Art might be thought of as an enrichment of Mathematics, as this group of children was selected primarily for intellectual ability and not for creativity.

The personal preparation for the work took the form of recalling encounters with people who might have been described as "gifted" students, friends, colleagues and children. They were considered in relation to experiences in Art and Craft and also to extracts from an article by Margaret Mead [38]. Margaret Mead's statements that she considered "the gifted child needs scope, inconspicuous access to books, museums, instruments, paints, ideas to feed himself from the genius of other ages . . . contact, however fleeting, with those who are masters in the abilities with which he has been specially endowed . . . and "an explicit sanction against selling his birthright for a mess of pottage . . ." seemed to be a reasonable starting point, raft and guide. Now, nearly three years later, it would seem that in addition the young gifted child needs the sincere and constant interest of an informed adult, who is without prejudice and inflexible attitudes of mind. Some mature students, often parents themselves, at first find it hard to realize that, in some fields, an eight-year-old can see, think or reason more clearly than they can themselves. It is a salutary experience for grown-ups to work with these children, and such children are fortunate indeed if the grown-ups who live and work with them are truly adult.

From the beginning it was agreed that the staff of each subject would listen and take part in the other's lessons. There was a natural friendliness from the children when an adult was doing the same work as they were, sometimes even at a lower level. Students were encouraged to join in, even if it was not "their subject." From time to time both subjects needed to move away from a common area, each into the core of its own sphere, returning with new experiences into double-harness when suitable. Mutual understanding grew easily in these conditions; without it integration would have been impossible.

That Art and Mathematics would make a good unit was accepted from the start, but not until the end was it realized that they needed each other. This was later reaffirmed—perhaps obliquely—by the first two books of the Nuffield Mathematics Project, where the quotation "One picture is worth a thousand words" is referred to and where the need for recognizing "patterns within relationships" is linked with aesthetic quality. Visual perception which is developed in Art when children are encouraged to look and analyse by drawing or modelling would seem to be an educable aspect of awareness. The seeing of a whole relationship which may alter the tone or colour of a part, is part of visual awareness and is paralleled in Mathematics. Most of all, Art needs to be envisaged as a subject that uses thought as well as intuition, while Mathematics requires the creative handling of tools and materials, as well as mental activity.

The general idea behind the Art, at the start, was that it should give every opportunity for growth in visual perception and experience with many materials. To this end it was planned that during the first year a variety of approaches and problems would be presented as a seeding for later recall. Sometimes, the visual and tactile work might prepare the ground, as was foreseeable in Symmetry, sometimes it might reinforce an experience. In the early days the children could not remember the word "parabola" although they could draw one and knew what it was. A soft, attractive toy monkey, with wire in its limbs, was brought in for them to play with among other toys. It was called "Parabola" and they made it sit and swing in life-like positions—they drew it later swinging from binary tree to binary tree! A year or more later in a different building one boy was overheard to say, with pleasurable recognition, "Oh look, there's Parabola!"

The experiment started with thirteen children selected from three schools. The Art material which was taken in to establish an interesting environment—shades of Margaret Mead—included toys such as roundabouts, kaleidoscopes, moveable wooden animals and hexa-flexagons for them to pattern; a branch of the large variety of Spurge (Euphorbia) for binary form; and books. Knowing, now, how they work their way round the College Art and Craft room, commenting and examining everything, one can only assume that at first they were inundated, as little interest was shown.

Their first practical job was to tear a Y shape—the binary diagram—from coloured-supplement paper, and then to tear the shape through four thicknesses of paper to make four similar shapes. These were then pinned on to a piece of soft-board to make a circular, symmetrical pattern. Their main comment was, why could they not have scissors, as they disliked tearing! Later we found that "liking" was often related to lack of experience and a fear of not doing well. Most took paper home to make a small design of their own. The following week, however, when they were asked to tear their initials to stick on to their folders, they were stumped. They could draw, but could not tear the letters which were not symmetrical. This was overcome. Conversation earlier had revealed interesting backgrounds and experiences in Maths; so we talked. Only two of the girls had made "doilys" but the idea of folding attracted them all. Newspapers were used and experiments were made—this time with scissors—on the principle of "Can you fold it differently?" "What happens if you fold and re-fold?" and so on. They took home small squares of coloured tissue paper but only a few came back. The double factor of overlapping holes and transparency was not really appreciated. When this work was recalled over a year later it was taken by a student who asked them to make banners or pennons, and was very successful.

The need for being able to visualize, to imagine, to see in the mind's eye was apparent and necessary in both subjects so the Art work was directed to this end for the next few weeks. Tulips were taken in—but not out, and they were asked to imagine the cross-section of a half-cut tulip showing the pattern of pistil and stamens against a background of petals. Czechoslovakian papercuts were then shown and they were asked to "see" or imagine the flower in the round. Coloured papers were then selected by them and after folding, they cut three different sections in diminishing sizes and super-imposed them to form a flower head. They were eager to cut more at home, so the symmetrical bowl of flowers was not organized and gummed into place until the following week. They were now familiar with the binary diagram but when they saw a branch in binary form in the round they were unable to recognize it.

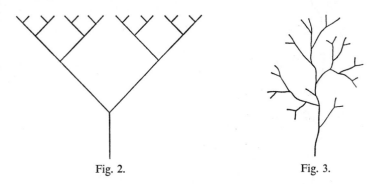

Fig. 2.   Fig. 3.

Only one or two could "play" with their seeing. They had all stroked a cat, but had not seen the invisible line in the air which was the shape of the cat made by the movement of their hands. They knew the phrase "a bird's eye view," but had not played at seeing as a bird. During this phase it was realized that even if they did visualize or give a word to a visual symbol their word or symbol was not always common to others.

To try to develop their facility for this type of imaginative seeing we asked them to carry out an exercise which was in the nature of an experiment. This exercise involved presenting them with ten shapes to which they had to assign appropriate words or names, and also with ten words for which they had to draw ten appropriate shapes. (These words and shapes appear on pages 108-9.) The results were most revealing and did help them, to some extent, to develop their imaginative faculties.

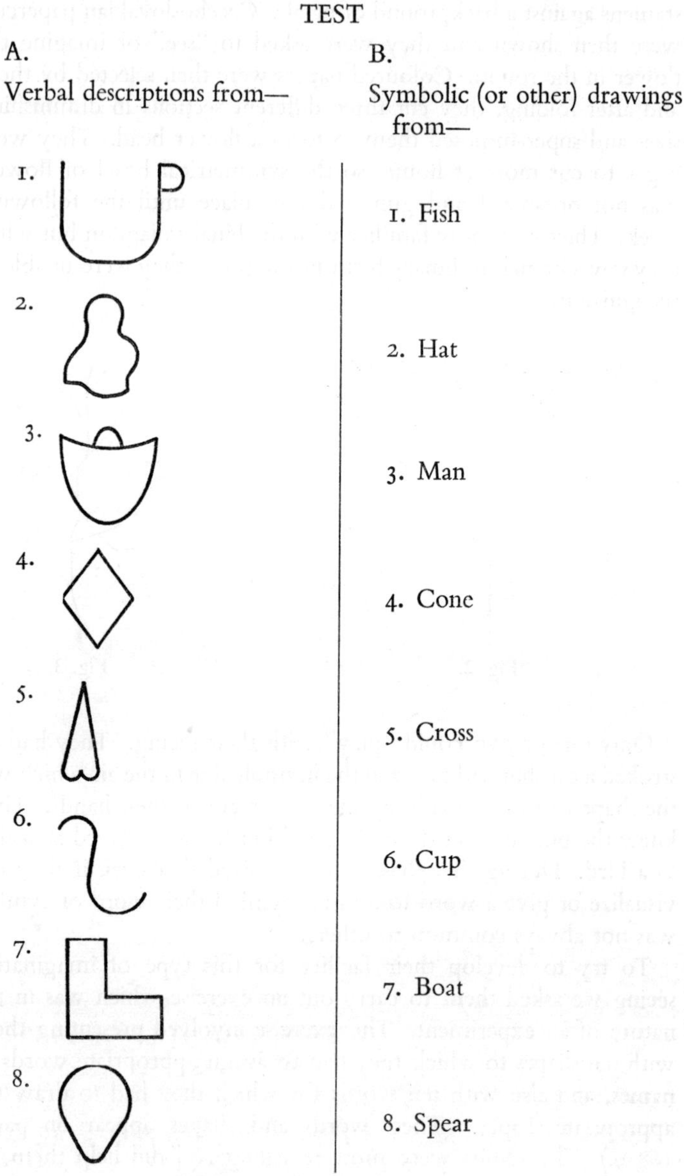

TEST

A.	B.
Verbal descriptions from—	Symbolic (or other) drawings from—

1.

2.

3.

4.

5.

6.

7.

8.

1. Fish

2. Hat

3. Man

4. Cone

5. Cross

6. Cup

7. Boat

8. Spear

Fig. 4.

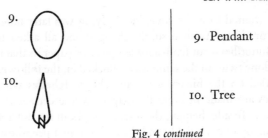

9.

10.

9. Pendant

10. Tree

Fig. 4 *continued*

The most subtle drawings and most descriptive words came from two of the children who were most creative and interested in Art and Craft. Not one of them knew the word "pendant." It was interesting to note than an oval shape was called a circle, a lemon, an orange, and an apple—but not an egg. In the meantime they made binary trees with nine pipe cleaners. One pipe cleaner bound the trunk and the eight were then divided, twisted and sub-divided, once, twice and again to make branches. The trees were dipped in dye and with selected stones, rock and gravel made into a *Thunderbird* landscape which could be viewed from many points of view. It was hoped to lead on to drawing from these contacts but, before this could be attempted by all, considerable reassurance had to be given to a few.

They were intelligent children, so an approach was made through reason. It was explained that Art required thought, like Mathematics. The Greeks and the Egyptians, the Persians and the Italians were renowned for both Art and Mathematics. Art and Craft was illimitable. If one aspect was too difficult or failed to please, all that was needed was to ask for something else.

A range of individual work was organized, with the needs of those who required help in mind. Work cards went with small boxes which contained materials, stimulus and illustrative matter. Pattern-making by drawing around cut shapes, which were capable of many arrangements, overcame an assumed (or conditioned) inability to draw. They were encouraged to look at books instead of "doing any work"; to play with toys or use the reflecting kaleidoscope all round the room; to go on with Maths, if they so wished. The effort made to reassure the few was even more appreciated by those who really did not need it and the new system was taken to its limits. The limits just included the last request,

"Well I really wanted to make rope," and plying was later taught to all. The attitude to Art had subtly changed and all asked for homework. Butterflies—cut from a folded piece of paper so that no lineshape was done twice in the same way—flocked in, the following week, and settled on the binary tree—an echo of Rhodes where tourist brooches are made in butterfly shapes because certain trees attract butterflies. Besides helping the few, the work in the different boxes opened many doors quickly and the children met peepshows, three-dimensional work in card, the use of hemp, string, wool, Plasticine, problems with mirrors and various kinds of pattern making. Above all they saw work in Art and Craft as problems to be solved and not as mindless occupation with the materials only.

Colour work with water was not easy at this stage but some mixing and matching was attempted. There was little sustained interest, however, and anxiety returned in case the work was spoiled or the paint boxes were not kept clean. As Easter was near the problems of the mother of the Cave twins [16] were considered. She knew about nests, and could make rope out of grasses (as could the children) but for her way of life she needed such things that later would be called baskets, cradles, boats, shoes and coffins. She had to think, experiment and learn from her mistakes. The children made birds' nests with varying degrees of competence from the willow, honeysuckle, iris leaves and other pliable materials from the garden. As true children, however, their greater interest was in the little, coloured eggs.

Discussions that followed later in the year suggested that the one word which did not have a common meaning for all was Art. Craft was to them a short course on Basketry or Boatmaking. They agreed that thinking resulted in wanting, seeing and doing; doing needed a medium or material, and the following list of materials had counterpart occupations in adult life—

Paints, pencils, paper, etc.	Illustrators, painters, etc.
Wood, stone, metal, etc.	Architects, sculptors, carpenters, engineers, etc.
Clay, Plasticine, plaster.	Potters, mosaicists, builders.
Yarns, fibres.	Weavers, Fabric designers, etc.

Natural materials and derivatives. Manufacturers of all kinds.

They agreed that the words "Art and Craft" could include, in schools, such a range of thought and materials.

Their experiences had included the use of various kinds of paper; coloured crayons, paint and inks; hemp, wire, and garden fibres. Hessian was now given to them in small squares, first of all to unravel the edges and then to pull out and replace threads in the warp and weft. They were asked if they could make patterns using other colours or yarns, or how they could fill the hole left where the original warp and weft crossed. The scale of the work was too small for them to manipulate easily, so fleece was used thickly, and cross-way strips of selected materials from rag-bags were woven into netting. When this was recalled a year later, a student asked them to make pendant designs on netting, using plyed and woven materials. They were all different and yet within the terms of reference.

A tentative return was made to drawing, where before there had been lack of confidence. Observation of the thundery, stormy skies was discussed and relationships of whites or greys compared. Verbal descriptions were tried, and pictures by Turner and Constable were shown. "Noah's ark in the flood" was drawn and coloured with crayons by all, without anyone making a comment or hesitating. The results were most interesting. As a contrasting activity, they were given a large plastic bag each, which contained the following materials: card, fabric, thin sticks of bamboo, short pieces of dowelling, paper fasteners, several short lengths of wool, newspaper and cotton wool. They were asked only "What can you make?" There was no anxiety. On the contrary, it was great fun. It had been intended to reassure them after a minute or two, but this was quite unnecessary. No one was stumped, and the objects made included several boats, a baby in a cot, fish in a pond, a house in a tree, a Punch and Judy show, and a snow scene. The work was then taken over by a student who was interested in fabric pictures and the children came to the Harold Court outpost of the College, and worked in the Art and Craft room there for the rest of their time with us. This room, a hut in an old apple orchard, with verandas outside and moveable tables inside, offers an ideal situation for this type of work. There is nothing that cannot be moved, adapted or exploited for experimental work in both subjects—and nothing that can be damaged!

Another project was started at a time when the Fire of London was being recalled on posters. The first job was paper-cutting and the making of a picture of a bonfire. The visual image was started by building in front of them, with short lengths of cut branches, a small fire. The lighting and burning of the fire was mimed and described in visual language. All the children set to work, and, apart from being encouraged to work on a larger scale by joining their paper-cut flames, they needed no help. Many remembered the colours of the flames they had seen in science, and most took the unused scraps of coloured paper back to school. The following week, many of them brought back commemorative stamps they had made, from the scraps, for the occasion—an exercise in miniature.

Colour work arose first in the science lesson with mixing paints, and the lesson did not change—only the emphasis was put on matching colours around in the room and seeing what new colour was next to the one matched. Heat, water, buoyancy and buildings, in science, offered scope for mobiles, pattern work, cardboard villages and stories. Frank Lloyd Wright was referred to, and one of the children found out more about him during the week. Earthquakes linked science with legend, and the children were told the story of Theseus, the Minotaur, and Sir John Evans's experiences of a noise like a bull roaring during an earthquake in Crete. An interesting point now arose over recording observations, and telling the truth. The class was asked to draw a flag (a rectangle with two diagonals) without either taking the pencil off the paper or going over a line twice. It cannot be done. Two children maintained, even in the face of proof, that they had done it. Their visual work, even when based on observation, was still being drawn at a conceptual level. They would tell in words the true facts about the windows in the house opposite the school, but they painted the house as they had painted houses before, in the Infant School. It seemed reasonable to approach this problem, and an attempt was made through visual channels.

The children were asked if they had ever told a lie, and before they could really answer they agreed that if they told little lies adults said that they were telling fibs (*Oxford Dictionary*, "fable") or stories. They all knew that stories began "Once upon a time . . ." Talk then centred on "time." A piece of wallpaper about 20 foot long had been folded into halves, quarters, eighths and sixteenths. It was kept folded so that the children could see the first hundred years only—from 1966 back across time to 1866. Each section was 100 years. The paper was opened out, section by section, to three divisions, to the Fire of London. They all knew 1066 from the posters at that time for Guinness! It seemed a long piece of paper, however, when nine divisions were opened out, and it was quite understandable that stories told over that length of paper/time could alter the truth and become fables or legends. The birth of Christ was also further back than was expected, and Theseus was off the end of the paper, which now required the support of four children. The class-teacher nobly co-operated here by taking the *ten* similar 20-foot sheets back to school, where, in a windy play-ground, the children could see, even on this scale, how long a time ago were the bulls painted in the caves at Altamira and Lascaux.

A parallel exercise in the observation and painting of houses was taken with the gifted children at the Harold Court outpost. A comparison of the results showed a marked difference between ability to memorize and ability to organize structure before detail. All the gifted children understood the analysis of the view, and it was interesting to see their treatment of the skies.

The work with the class of unselected children continued with verbal descriptions and observation and with actual handling of a very docile white rabbit. Very good results were obtained in colour from observation, but ideas through words were not so easily translated. Meanwhile, work in science included mirrors and reflections. In art, three mirrors, each 1 foot square, were arranged to stand so that they formed an equilateral triangle with the reflecting surfaces inside. The children were given similar sized triangular pieces of paper, and from selected fabric, which they could cut as they wished, they made informal patterns. These patterns, when placed inside the three reflecting mirrors, gave a field of repeats. Through this repeating all-over pattern, the children could at once see weaknesses of grouping and accent. Some very subtle patterns were made later by the gifted children.

At the end of this period of two terms of dual experiment, it was realized that the class of unselected children was easier to teach. The presence of the class-teacher was of great value, but, unlike the gifted children, attitudes towards the subjects were not so firmly established. The gifted children had to learn that handwork was necessary for experimental work in Mathematics (see Chapter 9) and that mistakes and failures did not matter. In both groups there was evidence of anxiety when an inability to draw was experienced, but in the class of unselected children it was less, and very easily overcome.

At the Harold Court outpost students were completely in charge of art with the gifted children. That all was well was shown by their work and co-operation, and by such conversations with the gifted children—

"Hallo, how are you getting on at Harold Court?"
"Oh, we're having a lovely time. We're working on computers and making papier mâché birds."

Was there a possibility that Art was being accepted wholeheartedly, and the seeding of the first year was beginning to put out roots?

Pattern had been touched upon in three different aspects. One, when a practical link had been made between the principle of the adding machine and potato cuts; again when swinging pendulums made invisible lines in the air; and also when large mirrors had been used to show all-over repeats. When tessellating patterns were taken in Maths, the Art work followed by exploring similar problems in coloured paper-cuts, starting from the chequer board. It was found that if a single piece was cut off and rejoined to a dark square—and of course repeated with all the other dark squares— a tessellation might or might not occur. If the square was folded and two identical pieces were cut and replaced against it symmetrically, a tessellation resulted, but was not always recognized by the children, if the total shape went across the colours.

A study was made of an Alhambra tile (Fig. 5), and it became visually evident that the line drawn from N to E was the same line as that from S to E (Fig. 6). How did the line in Fig. 7 differ? The children were asked to describe this line in words, but until they became climbers (steep slope and across the plain) they could not think of words. Any line could now be imagined and tessellated shapes made which repeated in four ways; before, the earlier patterns had repeated only in parallel. Progression was made

Fig. 5.

by a few who applied their knowledge to a triangular and an hexagonal grid, the best one of which was done at home.

M. C. Escher in his *Graphic Work* [7] comments on the fact that the Moors were past masters of designs "of an abstract geo-metrical type," and regrets that "not one single Moorish artist . . . ever made so bold . . . as to use . . . recognisable, naturistically

Fig. 6.   Fig. 7.

conceived figures of fish, birds, reptiles or human beings in their surface coverage." Such a shape, with its visual knowledge modified to obey the laws of mathematics, takes some time to evolve and requires a development from conceptual form to observational realism.

This was the period when the children did not know whether the subject of the lesson was Art or Mathematics, or both! The naming of a period is a barrier as well as a help, and the walls need breaking down at times.

At the end of this term it was decided to put out a half-hundred-weight block of prepared clay. The clay was on a zinc tray on a table. The children were given work-cards asking such questions as "Can you make a tunnel?" "Can you make an imprint?" "Can you make two contrasting textures?" "What else can you make?" They poked, they tunnelled and they talked. How we wished we had had a tape recorder! Their questions would have given us a year's work in clay and pottery techniques alone; as was, their comments ranged from skeletons to temperatures, from clay deposits in Cornwall to China, Persia and Egypt, from foot-prints to marbles! They later glazed their marbles, and for them glaze will mean putting their hands into wet, cold, thick liquid as well as the shine on pots.

The idea of free choice was discussed, and for a week or two they were offered options, but finally, after such questions as, "Do you prefer to work alone?" "Would you like to choose your starting point or subject each week?" the answers were always "Yes *and* No." They wanted to be left alone but they wanted us there. They wanted to choose but they also wanted to see what we had to offer—so—we taught them the word "compromise" and they savoured it and used it.

Toys were still a stimulus at different levels. Small gold-net bags containing miniature villages in coloured wood were played with happily, but when it was suggested that if arranged on a large sheet of paper they already had the knowledge of arranging roads and paths in such a way that each building could be separately numbered and identified, they thought for a minute or two, discussed it among themselves, murmured "binary?" and then set to work, and made maps. This exercise later was approved by the Geography staff, as the children drew round the bases of the little wooden buildings, thus making ground plans.

Many had the game of Spirograph, so in September narrow off-cuts of heavy cylindrical card were nailed around the circumfer-ences so that envelopes of string could be taken across in patterns. It was found that 91 nails gave a seven-pointed shape in conjunction with a thirteen-faceted envelope; 96 was full of triangular and square possibilities. This fringe area of play was enjoyed by staff, students and children, and led to geometry and pattern-making in colour with circles. It was now possible for them to draw accurately the Persian tile in the form of a Y which they had played with earlier. This they may meet again in the Benaki Museum in Athens or in the Edward VII Gallery of the British Museum. It is personally thought that by considering the creative use of materials only in Art, the fringe areas that link with other disciplines may be forgotten, thus missing much Art, which in our heritage is held in mosaics, basketry, weaving, wood and stone carving and embroidery, as well as in painting.

Students continued for a time to give the children opportunities for more observational drawing, until it was realized that there were still some children who did not see all that could be seen, even in an objective still-life. To help this, a large assortment of circular and rectangular objects was placed on the floor on two large drawing-boards. The bottles and bricks were so placed that not one actually touched another, but the spaces in between were varied. By walking round and rearranging it was possible to make five opportunities where the light wood of the drawing board could be seen as an enclosed shape. The children were asked to find—

    (i) An isolated bottle with board all round (very easy).
and (ii) An isolated piece of board with bottle edges (or brick, etc.) all round.

They were then asked to *say*—read—the shape in words. This was then drawn by them in the air with their eyes shut, and then repeated on paper. Thus the words, "long slope, down a little way at right angles, small curve to right, slope back to left but not so far as first line, straight up, curve left and up to starting point," made this shape (Fig. 8) which was explained by further observation, to this (Fig. 9):
In this way, drawing by eye is always cross-checked and confidence is given. It requires effort however. A diversion followed, with making Mobius strips, which offered further opportunities for seeing shapes in between, as well as doing work in three dimensions.

By this time the children belonged to the room, and their work was displayed in it as well as the students' work. Both were interested in each other's problems and tried some of them out practically. With some knowledge of circles, the children rolled cheap paper into short rods and were asked: "Can you make a sphere by joining the rods with Sellotape?" One of the solutions, which developed an envelope from rods at right angles to radii, impressed the students, as they too had used such materials and had now a respect for the difficulties of the media.

In the last Summer the children were with us, some students were considering an old Hoover in relation to a project on Wind. The children enjoyed playing with bubbles as much as the students.

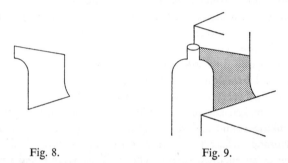

Fig. 8.   Fig. 9.

In Mathematics, pertinent questions were asked, and it was hoped that at last all of them would be able to visualize the invisible air currents, but difficulty was still found in this area. It was not until a small speck of invisible air was called "Fred" that the route of the bubbles was seen and the returning air route to the Hoover imagined. Perhaps we were asking too much. Even the Greeks took it in steps, as the description of a torso of a young girl whose dress is blowing in the wind shows (Figure of a personified breeze National Museum, Athens). "Figure" is a statement of the obvious; "personified" is a warning before the invisible is suggested and then seen in the dress.

As a final exercise, the children painted or drew their portraits from a long mirror. Not that we needed to be reminded of their faces. We had worked with them for nearly three years and from them had learned. It was to us a most enjoyable experience.

11 *The Approach through Science*

STANLEY G. FISHER, B.Sc.

THE work with children during the four years under consideration has been mainly, though not totally, concerned with those members of the larger group who had expressed a specific interest in scientific activities, and whose responses and abilities may well have little general applicability. It is interesting to note however that this type of activity may be a preference of many gifted children [14]. It was certain that the children had a specific understanding and hope that the activity for which they had opted would involve much "messing about with test tubes and apparatus," and in addition the term Science, as used in Primary education, is frequently used so as to exclude much biological work [33].

It seems appropriate therefore at this stage to define, if possible, the nature and scope of science and to list some of the objectives of science teaching, so that the attributes of these children may be seen in perspective.

A student survey carried out at Brentwood has shown that there are many interpretations of the area of scientific activity and many more of the scientific process. These ranged from "a study of everything that is in the world" to facts, facts and nothing but! Clearly there is a need for something more specific.

The area of operation may be said to be the natural world (only to exclude supernatural phenomena), but what is more helpful is to look at the processes involved, in short to arrive at some general statement of the Scientific Method. Michael Bassey [4] gives as a justification for the teaching of science "science in its description and harmonising of the natural world is a part of our material environment; because science in its concern for ideas and models of the natural world is a part of our intellectual environment; and because the method of science is a powerful tool for unravelling secrets and *solving problems.*" And further, "children are instinctively curious, and science offers an unrivalled opportunity for the teacher to nourish that curiosity."

There are clear implications here of opportunities for the display of intellectual qualities of considerable range and variety, and that science may be defined as those fields of human activity posing problems which may be tackled by application of the scientific method. The scientific method is one of a number of problem-solving processes among which are the use of logic, common sense and intuition, but it is distinguished from them (not to their exclusion) by the need for the solution of a problem to be based on verifiable observations and measurements. Leonardo da Vinci wrote: "I shall begin by making some experiments before I proceed any further; for it is my intention first to consult experience and then to show by reasoning why that experience was to turn out as it did . . . experience never errs, what alone may err is our judgment, which predicts effects that cannot be produced in our experiments."

The search for pattern amongst the mass of information which constitutes our factual observations daily takes us to the abstract, to the realm of ideas, and involves imagination and creativity. James Clark Maxwell wrote in 1855 that "the first process in the effectual study of science must be one of simplification and reduction of results of previous investigation to a form in which the mind can grasp them. The result of this simplification may take the form of a purely mathematical formula or of a physical hypothesis."

The word "hypothesis" is introduced here and requires some illustration. Johann Wolfgang von Goethe wrote: "Hypotheses are the temporary bridges that a scientist constructs along his mental pathway between initial curiosity and later acceptable understanding," and "Hypotheses are the scaffolds which are erected in front of a building and removed when the building is completed. They are indispensable to the worker; but he must not mistake the scaffolding for the building."

A fruitful hypothesis has a most essential characteristic in that it suggests further experiments, the results of which will bring about modification or even rejection. Imagination produces hypotheses, but it is observation which holds the hypothesis to reality.

Before concluding this brief statement with a summary of the scientific method, it seems wise to repeat McKenzie's warning, "much nonsense is talked about the scientific method, which is regarded as a kind of mystique, like the American Way of Life or the British Constitution. There are no Queensberry Rules for investigators of nature and no holds should be barred" [36]. Nevertheless there are certain fundamental features which describe the usual approach of a scientist to a problem which is capable of being so treated.

Scientific Method

(i) Define the problem (i.e., ask a specific question).

(ii) Collect observations (facts) relevant to the problem (and carefully record).

(iii) Arrange the facts until some pattern or apparent solution to the problem arises—hypothesis construction.

(iv) Test the idea against the known facts. If it is supported, collect further information by means of the experiments suggested by the hypothesis and modify or reject as required.

(v) Communication of the hypothesis by any means which is appropriate (written and spoken word, mathematical symbols, illustrations, models, etc.).

The discussion so far has been concerned with definitions, but we must ask ourselves how it is related to the needs of children. It has been said that "the stimulation of curiosity and wonder at natural phenomena, and the recognition of science as a major human activity, should find a place in the education of all children." But what is possible in practice? Is the attitude and method of the trained scientist something which is foreign to children? Should we be satisfied with merely descriptive teaching (i.e., information) about the natural world? Are there certain limited aspects of the scientific method which are well suited to children's abilities from the earliest age? In this respect, is the gifted child able to extend the process further than would normally be expected?

These questions have been insufficiently examined as yet, but we do have some evidence which will allow us to proceed, but not, of course, to come to any conclusion.

It would be generally agreed that young children need to be involved in many real and practical situations; this indeed is the present position in most parts of the curriculum.

The Nuffield Foundation Junior Science Teaching Project has stated seven basic premises about children, the first two of which are—

(i) They must be given as much concrete experience as possible.
(ii) They must be encouraged to ask questions, and their questions and answers must be treated with respect, otherwise they will be reluctant to ask any more.

The first of these premises may be thought to be derived from the work of Piaget and, as a basic requirement of Primary work, is closely related to the preliminary phases of the scientific method. Unusual curiosity has been said to be an acknowledged characteristic of the gifted [14 and 52]. Nevertheless, the second premise contains a warning to those responsible for the gifted. The Nuffield team went on to say that "children have a natural curiosity about their environment and they satisfy this curiosity by methods which are essentially scientific. Their curiosity and short-lived interest in any particular topic causes them to turn quickly from one problem to another, often an unrelated one, and the result is a rapidly growing collection of data which may remain unconnected for some time, but without which it will be impossible to have any understanding of the underlying general principles of science which come later." Perseverance and tenacity in dealing with difficult topics have been said to be an attribute of the gifted— these generalizations are difficult to deal with, but there does seem to be some supporting evidence.

It is believed, then, that children, especially the younger ones, need real problems which can be dealt with by means of concrete experience and that this will lead to scientifically meaningful questions. All children deserve a school environment which is rich in materials and potentialities for such investigation—this may be an accentuated need for the gifted.

There is an interesting by-product of such a situation. Discovery sparks off the desire to communicate and provides excellent opportunities for talking, writing, diagram-making and so on. Gifted children love to use long words correctly [52] and on some occasions to display this ability for adult visitors [33]. And yet many of us feel ourselves unable to undertake such work; we feel ourselves ill-equipped to answer the questions which the children are certain to ask. Hence the proper demand for more in-service courses which deal with scientific background and for more attention to this matter in the initial training of teachers. The Nuffield team had an important point to make here, "the great doubt felt by many teachers has been their own lack of scientific training, and there is often the feeling that they could do much better if they themselves knew more about the topic under discussion. To try to allay these fears, the project is producing a series of background information booklets for teachers, but our experience is that scientific knowledge is not the answer. The problem seems to be solved as soon as a teacher has sufficient confidence to say to a child: 'I don't know the answer, but let us sit down and work out together how we can find one'" [6]. (The answer brings with it no loss of face. Indeed it is a truly scientific attitude and, in any case, no one could give a definite answer to many of the questions which are asked.) The demand for background information is understandable but does contain certain elements of danger. Nevertheless, children do demand answers and is it reasonable to expect that a gifted boy who is able to give a detailed and explicit description of the electronics of a television camera will expect less?

There is no shortage, now-a-days, of suitable books and sources of information for teachers who wish to undertake work in this area with young children; one book, the U.N.E.S.C.O. Sourcebook for Science Teaching [50] deserves a special mention as a valuable source of experimental information which could be used to create rich situations for inquiry.

Even so, it is worth repeating that the attitude of the teacher and the atmosphere in the classroom are of the first importance. The experience which a young teacher takes into the classroom is very much the concern of the Colleges of Education, and the situation seems to be improving rapidly. Nevertheless, undesirable physical features of many classrooms make a potentially rewarding atmosphere difficult to attain. A water supply and a source of heat are sometimes provided but are frequently absent. Both these problems can be overcome without great difficulty, using plastic containers and portable heat supplies up to and including bottled gas burners. Children's desks with flat, horizontal tops, are becoming common, and can be grouped to produce good working areas. Storage space is usually limited but very necessary, as indeed is room for an interest (work) table which may take the form of a narrow bench (about 18 inches wide) running along the window side of the classroom. Display space for charts, illustrations and result sheets should be provided. Mains electricity should be avoided and most work can be done with a supply of dry batteries, although a disused car battery can be a useful acquisition even if rather cumbersome. All of these things are possible, but the problem of overcrowded classrooms is not easily dealt with. Space is vital if the children are to be directly involved, but compromise may be the only answer when elbow room is just not available. Far more of the practical work will have to take the form of child-assisted teacher-executed activities which can be useful, provided we avoid a reversion to demonstration and verification as opposed to investigation and discovery. There are, of course, occasions when direct teaching is the proper approach. Is this more or less so in the work with gifted children?

Very little commercial scientific equipment is needed; most of the apparatus can be assembled out of material obtained from the local ironmonger, from the kitchen, from the home. The Nuffield team considered that "home-made apparatus, make-do-and-mend materials, and bits and pieces are phrases which aptly describe the kind of apparatus associated with Primary school science, and there are good reasons for it. First the financial aspect must not be ignored. If the children are to do individual work, the cost of buying apparatus can be prohibitive. It would also lead to careful selection and a rapidly predetermined course of study based on the apparatus the teacher decided to buy. But a more important reason is to encourage children to look at science not as a subject to be done at special times in special rooms, using special apparatus, but as a way of discovering, which can be applied anywhere, at any time, with whatever materials happen to be available. If he has become dependent on a supply of traditional scientific apparatus before he can work in a scientific way, the discoveries the child is likely to make about the world are likely to be severely restricted. Perhaps the most important reason for home-made equipment is the understanding gained by the child in designing and constructing it."

In addition to the U.N.E.S.C.O. Sourcebook and the Nuffield Project literature, both of which give considerable information with respect to home-made apparatus and to materials required, we have made use of four handbooks published by the Association for Science Education, *Science for Primary Schools* [2].

It seems appropriate to point out that the Nuffield work was concerned with the day to day activities in the Primary school, and it has recently been suggested that more attention might have been given to the very able children. Is it likely that the progress of the gifted child when given such opportunities may sooner or later bring the need for more precise equipment?

There is also the question of timetables and of what allocation of time would be appropriate for scientific work in the Primary school. This proposition is based on a presumption that the kind of science we have suggested is best treated in isolation. This would not seem to be so as children may need to see the environment as a whole and much of the work could grow out of other subjects, ideally when the interest is at its height. Do gifted children show the opposite trend towards intense concentration and convergence in their scientific activities? In any case, is true science and discovery most likely to be fostered by convergent or divergent thinking? Perhaps there is no single answer to such questions.

Two further aspects need to be mentioned, that concerned with the use of books and also the question of communication of results and records. Firstly, books: books are one of the science teacher's most helpful teaching aids. They can provide him with a great deal of background information and can assist him in presenting the material in the most successful way; they will, of course, be books written for adults. But books are, perhaps, of most value when available for reference by the children and when so used can broaden discoveries made in the classroom, and on occasions may give rise to initial problems and questions. They should be colourful, well made, clearly illustrated and authoritative. An index and a bibliography are essential and of particular importance are those of the single topic type (or monograph). Books to be avoided are those that give the results of experimental work which children could perform themselves.

Are books likely to be a stimulus to scientific investigation, or, on the other hand, is scientific inquiry likely to promote the use of the school or local library? Again, no single answer is likely, but this is clearly a question which should be investigated with particular reference to very able children. *Science for Primary Schools No. 2 List of Books* [2] is a definitive reference when searching for suitable literature on children's investigations as they occur.

The second aspect concerned the reporting of experimental work. What written work should be required from child investigators? What is our objective in requiring written reports? Accurate recording and communication are vital parts of the scientific process, but here there may be a danger. Is much of what we do, in this respect, accurate recording of real observations? Should we allow written work to become pre-eminent in what is, above all, an exciting practical investigation? Is there a case for imaginative interpretation using materials other than paper and pen? The Nuffield team concluded that children should be encouraged to communicate their discoveries immediately and in whatever medium they consider suitable at the time. On the other hand it could be considered that simple scientific work can provide opportunities from which reading and writing first develop. The need for new words often becomes acute—"solution" is an example of this. Are gifted children more able and willing to commit their ideas and discoveries to paper in an orderly and worthwhile manner?

In all that has been said up to this point, we have been concerned almost entirely with the initial stages of scientific activity, the collection of data, the posing of questions and the setting of problems. These activities would seem suitable and rewarding for children of all ages and ability ranges, but when are these concrete operational activities liable to begin to give way to the formal and more abstracted operations which are required when the need arises for hypothesis construction and testing? What is the frame-work of concepts appropriate to the age of these pupils? The Schools Council/Nuffield Project *Science* 5–13, who are extending the scope of the original Nuffield Project, have described their aims and objectives at three stages of development [9]. As an example—

Stage I	Stage II	Stage III
(approx. up to 9)	(approx. 9–11)	
Prediction of effect of change from observation of similar changes.	Appreciation of the need to control variables and use controls in investigations.	Selection of effective controls for testing hypotheses.

There is evidence that quite young children are able to create generalized ideas (hypotheses) from their observations; some ideas will be more valuable than others, but all should be taken seriously. It is not possible to generalize as to ages; in some situations this degree of formalization will occur and in others it will not. However, Primary school children more often than not will require adult support in seeing the implications of their ideas and creating testing situations (which are implicit in the most clearly stated generalizations.)

Do gifted children display a greater facility and imagination in creating generalizations? Does intuition play a greater role than normal? Do these very able children have the aptitude and willingness to put their ideas to the test using effective control situations? Is there a willingness to draw conclusions only on the evidence of experiments or observations, together with lack of bias from preconceptions?

These questions and many more of a similar nature have interested us, and our experiences will be described in the next chapter. No conclusions can be stated, owing to the limited nature of the study. Indeed, there is a high probability that complex questions of this form cannot have simple, categorical answers.

It seems appropriate to conclude this section with a statement made by Karl Pearson in 1892. "Does science, then, leave no mystery? On the contrary, it proclaims mystery where others profess knowledge."

12 Work with Gifted Children in Science

STANLEY G. FISHER, B.Sc.

THE activities at Brentwood over the years have mainly concerned children in the age range 8 to 11 years old with intelligence quotients, arrived at by various forms of testing, between 130 and 170+ on the Terman-Merrill test (1960) or 122 to 153 on the WISC, who had expressed a special interest in scientific activities. This interest had indeed been displayed by reading, experimenting or observing, far beyond what might be considered the normal activity of children at this age. It soon became apparent that considerable reading activity and an acutely developed memory were at least significant factors in their attitude to science. Too much significance should not be given to the fact that in the early stages few girls joined the science groups (the sample was very limited).

The main objective was concerned with student extended-course work, and was directed only towards student observation of and experience in working with very able children. Support and guidance were, of course, available from members of the tutorial staff, but essentially the planning and execution of the work was a student responsibility. Certain other objectives have emerged as our experience and knowledge of the aptitudes and needs of the children have increased, and, in the main, these have been concerned with the attitudes and responses of the children when placed in demanding situations requiring the imagination and creativity which lead to advanced concept formation about the physical world and to the more extreme stages of the scientific method. Until recently, little formal teaching had been indulged in, and much of the work was based on individual exploration and discovery, centered in

extremely rudimentary accommodation and using little manu-
factured science equipment—in short, a close reflection of the
circumstances in most Primary Schools. Of late, however, the
work has been carried out in fully equipped science laboratories,
and some considerable part of the work has required the active
participation of members of the science tutorial staff; there has
also been a small swing towards more highly structured and
guided teaching. On occasions, simple testing situations (agonizingly
difficult to devise and assess) have been set up. There have been no
conclusive findings, other than that, under ideal conditions, some
form of evaluation procedure would be a vital element in a large-
scale study of children, such as that contemplated by the Schools
Council/Nuffield Project *Science* 5–13 team at Bristol. When
considering some of the questions raised in the previous chapter,
it may be useful to give our impressions of the level of attainment
reached by the children at Brentwood relative to the three stages
of development proposed by the Bristol team. It would be expected
that in the main these children would have entered the final stage,
thought to be appropriate to children of a greater age (or, in some
cases, a stage not normally to be reached at all).

For example, "Forming the ideas of matter made up of particles
and some impressions about the size, number and movement of
these." There seemed no doubt, during a conversation of some
duration with a ten-year-old group, that ideas of the particulate
nature of matter were immediately available and ready for application in new situations. These concepts seemed to have been
arrived at intuitively and as a matter of faith (as indeed, in the final
analysis, there is little available first-hand evidence for a choice
between continuous and non-continuous material hypotheses).
These ideas are, of course, justified because of their usefulness,
and many of the children had clearly been accustomed to this
level of treatment in their reading. Having inadvertently described
exhaled air as oxygen, a tutor was corrected by one boy who
explained that the gas involved was carbon dioxide and that the
molecules consisted of one carbon atom placed centrally between
two oxygen atoms, the molecule being linear . . . and much more
in this vein. What is the proper response of a teacher in this situation? Certainly, to the tutor, it somehow seemed inappropriate

to investigate the nature of air and the process of burning, using candles and jam jars. And yet, may not these statements be merely factual recall of information derived from literature for which the boy had a great appetite? Was there any true understanding? There were many occasions when the individual investigation and discovery method seemed inappropriate. Individual conversations and practical sessions with the graduate chemist, to whom he was talking, seemed the appropriate answer, using all the resources of a fully equipped science department. This, of course, is not normally possible.

Gifted children are said to be inordinately curious; in general we have not found extreme examples of this and indeed, although there existed a desire to find out for one's self, there seemed no great preference for putting ideas to test before accepting or rejecting them, or indeed a spontaneous attempt to examine evidence critically. On occasions, decision making which was biased by pre-conceptions seemed to be yet another display of convergence in attitude. Even so, we are not convinced that this is other than a conditioned response which greater opportunity would not overcome. At times the scientific process does require a single-mindedness of purpose (perspiration as opposed to inspiration) but nevertheless many important and fruitful avenues can be missed through lack of ability to respond in other ways.

It is hoped in the future to combine library activities with those in science, in an attempt to evaluate which is the more likely to act as a stimulus to the other. There is a case to be made out for either approach, but it does seem that first-hand evidence initially, followed by directed and structured reading, has some merit, at the least.

A development from an appreciation of the need to learn the meaning of new words and use them correctly, through enjoyment in examining ambiguity in use of new words, to a preference for using words correctly in written descriptions, was noted. On the other hand, the conversational use of scientific terminology was highly developed and in general a preference for talking about their work should be compared with a fairly marked resistance to the written report. Results were noted where the value was apparent (notebooks were nevertheless frequently mislaid!) but neatness of

presentation was often absent. An investigation of subject preferences usually ranked literary and aesthetic activities with a very low
score, as these were not seen to be useful—shades of the Two
Cultures!

This desire to take an active part in discussion has led more
recently to a consideration of the factors which affect the pressure
of a gas, being treated in a semi-formal manner, and here was a
powerful demonstration of the advanced ability to separate
variables and exclude variables in the investigation of relationships.
Preconceptions were dealt with in a more immediate manner and
progress was very rapid; this topic involves mathematical concepts,
a subject which always occurred high in the list of preferences,
although sometimes the preference was actively denied!

These children need an active and flexible approach with the
ability on the part of the teacher to think quickly, as they often
grasp the point of an argument in what seems to be an intuitive
manner without requiring the same degree of development and
supporting evidence as is usual. This facility in concept formation
was, of course, not equally evident in all situations—on one
occasion there was a surprising difficulty in extending the idea of
capacity of hollow containers to the volume of solid objects,
required during an investigation of materials leading to classifica-
tion, in this particular case using the mathematical concept of
density.

The range of activities undertaken has been very great, and has
depended not only on the interests of the children but also to a
great extent upon the abilities and preferences of the students
involved—teacher security is clearly important, and the demand
for background information, which the Nuffield team noted, can
be an even stronger desire when working with the very able.
Nevertheless, it is a truism that for all teachers at some time in our
careers we are likely, sooner or later, to be called upon to help and
advise pupils or students whose intellectual gifts are far greater than
our own. This is not to say that we have nothing to offer in terms
of guidance, advice and, of course, all those attributes which
spring from our greater maturity.

It has been noted on many occasions that the gifted children were
often in the position of having created a useful hypothesis (often

cutting many corners in the process) but were not able, without guidance, to see the implications of their idea and how it might most simply be tested. This ability does seem to be connected, in some way, with maturity and experience, of which the teacher will have a fund on which to call. In science the most obvious testing situation is often not attainable, perhaps because the apparatus required is not available, the required situation is out of our grasp, suitable controls are not to be set up, and for many other reasons. Imagination is required here, but some suggestions can be beyond the normality, and far fetched!

It would seem perhaps an academic argument to discuss the relative importance of teacher as compared with apparatus and equipment in work of this nature. Perhaps it is sufficient to say that the possibilities seem extremely limited without adults to work with these children, whose gifts in terms of sympathy, under-standing, maturity and speed of thought are great (there was no place for the pedestrian student) and that the physical environment is of secondary importance. Even so, if the greatest help is to be made available to these high-flying children, an investment in terms of facilities will give considerable gain in the range of work possible.

The time allocation that students have been able to give to this work has been limited in the extreme. In most cases, an hour a week for one academic year, the project then being taken up by another group of students, with an inevitable variation in the quality of involvement and motivation. The absence of control groups is to be remarked upon—no scientific investigation this, but an observation period based on scientific activities as a vehicle. Control groups and objective testing situations were attempted by one student, and this statement in itself is merely an indication of the superior quality of the study on this occasion [33]. It would seem appropriate to quote a selection of extracts from the report which resulted from this study, for in this way some of the flavour, difficulties and rewards of this work may be estimated.

From the introduction: "At the outset of the study the ten boys were between 9 and 10 years old; 3rd year of Junior school. They were studied over a period of ten months, from May, 1966, to March, 1967, and this, with time taken for holidays, half-term breaks, Teaching Practice, etc., meant a total of approximately 24 periods, each of one hour."

The criteria for selection as "gifted": "Scores gained were between 130 and 155 on the WISC, 134 and 170+ on the Terman/ Merrill, and between 17 and 26 on the Watts/Vernon Test."

Work carried out: "The boys followed a wide programme of science work . . . of a kind generally carried out in Secondary Schools and the study followed a desire to emulate, in some way, the quality of response to problems, exercises, situations, etc., of these high-I.Q. children—to discover whether they were divergent or convergent. It was thought valuable to compare any findings with the response to the same situations made by less gifted children who were several years older: to discover, if possible, in what ways intelligence functioned, whether quality of 'output' was part of intelligence or experience."

And of testing procedures: "Four forms of test were selected: Test I . . . a model of a simple balance made by piercing a straw with a pin . . . the object of the exercise to assess the child's ability to grasp the essence of a problem. Test II . . . to devise a scale of measurements for the balance . . . object, to assess the ability of the child to reason. Test III . . . to discover something of the creativity of the boys, one of the Getzels and Jackson's Tests was used. Test IV . . . test of observation . . . presented with a stuffed fox and asked to describe it as fully as possible."

Of the control group: "They were in the upper range of a 'B' stream 4th-year Secondary form and each boy was 15 years old."

And of the actual testing: "The gifted boys did not read instructions carefully—they rushed ahead impetuously . . . visitors interrupted once or twice and offered unasked-for advice which spoilt the test and broke up the atmosphere. John panicked and became frightened that he was slipping behind. Charles played up to the visitors, calling out comments . . . could not get boys to work on own and not reason out loud . . . Ian drew the model and made calculations mentioning load arm and pivot . . . David swiftly set about fixing an effective scale . . . everybody had an idea of how to sort out the problem."

Of the older group of boys: "Nobody could fix a scale. These boys seemed less willing to accept the situation as it stood . . . they bent the situation to suit a known method . . . they did not stick to the point."

And, finally, a tentative conclusion: "Although the gifted boys could not solve the problem, once the general idea had been explained to them they understood how to solve it—they had grasped the principle."

Creativity testing gave inconclusive results with no great differentiation between groups. On the other hand, of observation testing: "the gifted boys were more accurate—their accounts were not as coloured by their feelings towards the animal."

Some general comments on the study included the following: "In some respects they were precocious and had lost much of the wonder which can be part of the charm of childhood (CAN THIS BE SAID TO HAVE A MORE GENERAL APPLICATION?) . . . to these boys there seemed little new—not that they had actually performed each task before—but because they grasped concepts quickly there seemed little naiveté about them. In play, however, they seemed much as any other 10–11 year old boys, with the same tendency to horseplay and to arriving late at a lesson because they had been climbing trees for conkers!" And in comparison, of the older boys: "Although bordering on manhood, they had a marked air of unsophistication."

The student says of the actual work carried out: "The boys enjoyed the work and readily grasped the object of the study. Identifying the flowers involved the use of a flora, reference to a variety of books on wild flowers, and the use of a hand lens. The study inspired Ian to start his own collection which he showed with great pride . . . he had collected and named 115 different specimens." Of the difficult working conditions: "When the laboratory was used for an exhibition, and so was unavailable, chemistry in the open air tended to get a little out of hand. However, efforts were made to test soil samples from the two sites for potassium, ammonium nitrogen, calcium, magnesium, phosphorus and nitrate nitrogen."

Of the boys' interests it was noted that: "It is in the Physics field of the natural sciences that the boys are most knowledgeable. Lessons to demonstrate natural phenomena would be wasting the time of these boys. Physical concepts seem to be so well understood by them—one might even suggest intuitively. It is felt that stretches of boredom might well face them in the future."

In conclusion, after some comments about the obvious limitations of the study and the practical difficulties involved: "It was not difficult to make sure that known requirements would be available, but almost impossible to anticipate that any side-tracks would be catered for—and these were possibly the greatest value of the work. However, for me the whole exercise has been worth while— as for the boys, they enjoyed it . . ."

These comments made by the student engaged in this work highlight some of the problems involved in organizing a small-scale study, but they may also indicate the very pressing questions which remain unanswered. Schools are under very great pressure, at this time, to include some scientific work and opportunities in the children's school day, and considerable support and advice are becoming available through various schemes and teaching projects. For the teacher whose class includes gifted children, this is perhaps the first task, and may go a long way, although perhaps not all the way, towards providing for the needs of the very able.

The need for children of Primary-school age to begin their education as scientists by having opportunities to observe, experiment and solve problems is now well accepted. We do not know just where or when the urge to be a scientist begins and, even if these children never become scientists in the professional sense, they will all live in a world organized and dominated by scientific ideas. It seems important that the chance to meet the scientific climate of thought from quite early years should be provided, or else the most favourable moment may go by. Children may not take up this line of thought, but all paths of human activity should be kept open, so that what begins as a random exploration of the world may lead to an ordered way of looking at it [15].

13 Experiments with a Class including Gifted Children

GEORGE MINIKEN, T.C.

ALMOST everybody, with the exception of those directly concerned, called them "creative" children, and two years later the title remained; but the meaning of the word "creative" is still even more obscure.

The children were Juniors, 7 to 8 years of age, a complete class, and split into two separate matched groups on the Raven's Matrices Test. This was an ordinary class of children, and, what has become important, they have remained ordinary, as children, but possibly very different in individual cases, as a result of our activities.

Looking back to the very beginning, even the reasons for working with these children have changed. Originally it was intended that a lecturer from Brentwood would work with the children, and be joined later by students, who would eventually take over responsibility completely; and the process was to be repeated elsewhere with a different group of students and children. Ideally, this would give the students an opportunity to work, experiment and develop their own knowledge of children, without the anxieties of failure, or lack of success, that often accompany students during training. The bad or unsuccessful lesson, or one out of control, could be as profitable to the student as the ordinary or even successful lesson, if only an honest analysis of the situation could be made. The lecturer too, with a new group of children, would have to accept the possibility of difficulties and failure despite experience and in the presence of students to be prepared to accept this. Provided both lecturer and students recognized the value of this possible situation, without either fearing loss of face, a healthy working relationship would form naturally.

We hoped we would learn something about children, perhaps even gain a specialist knowledge. We also felt that two subject specialists, normally working apart, might create an interesting working relationship, and in our case Art and Craft teamed up with Physical Education. Perhaps today we as specialists are a little more enlightened than we were two years ago, but at the time it was for us a new experience. A third consideration was to look into the meaning of creativity through working with children, and to find whether there was any link between creativity and intelligence.

The class of children was from a Junior School. The class-teacher accompanied them, and we worked together at an Infant School on Friday afternoons from 1.30 to 3.30. The Infant School had good, well-designed, bright classrooms, available because of a drop in population in the area, and had also developed as a Maths Centre. The school had a very good attitude to modern teaching and methods, and a sympathetic understanding of what we were trying to do, and was to become, later, very closely connected with our work. Although we did not fully appreciate the fact in the beginning, there was no doubt that our work with Juniors was a well-intentioned experiment—a case of finding out—but it was also a self-conscious effort on our part. However, when we looked at the Infants we found a natural way of teaching, and it was only when we conveyed this attitude of teaching into our Junior work that some kind of sincerity of purpose developed.

In theory our intentions were admirable, but in practice much that we hoped to do had to be abandoned. There were many reasons for this. Students can pass their examinations without having to experiment. Knowledge can be taken from books or from the experience of others. So those students who did spend Friday afternoons with us were the most serious and enthusiastic. Others who might have come along were unable to do so because of time-table commitments. But one felt a lack of communication, a lack of recognition of the value of what we were trying to do. Above all, we wanted stability, and to obtain this we had to rely on those who believed that what we were doing was worth while. This has to be said, and it is a sad reflection on our attitude to teaching, and to teacher training. It is a sobering thought also to those who believe that if we are to claim the status of profession-alism, of truly possessing knowledge, then we must at least include a knowledge of children, equally with, if not more than, a know-ledge of academic subjects.

From the very beginning, when our Juniors first arrived, their natural ways have remained constant, but we, the "experienced," "the grown-ups," have had to change and think again at regular intervals.

As specialists, we quite naturally worked separately, and split the afternoon into two, one period of movement and one of art.

We had not met the children previously, but because of our previous teaching experience we had on this first meeting a rather pleasant, perhaps even a successful afternoon.

Our first duty was to make contact with the children. We sat in a circle, exchanged names, and passed round a large quartz crystal. This formed the basis of a highly improbable story of a diamond found near the crown jewels and brought along especially for this first meeting. Now everybody knew about it, the problem was how to return it. This question brought a good many intense and concerned answers from the children, who either believed the story or wanted to believe it.

During this period of discussion, one child had spotted a human skull amongst several other objects, and, in a voice that brought all thoughts of diamonds and teachers' problems to an end, said, "My Daddy took me to a museum, and showed me a skeleton of a horse and a man, and said 'that skeleton could be your Grandad'." Everyone's attention was now concentrated entirely on the skull, and many questions followed: Was it real? Was it really some-body? Who was it?

This situation produced the first serious question we had to ask ourselves. If we wanted attention to remain with the diamond, what should we have done to avoid being side-tracked? If the children had been told earlier that at some period during the after-noon they would have to commit their ideas to paper, attention might have stayed with the diamond. But why should we not accept that for one or more children the skull was of more interest than the diamond? We adults usually have a choice. In fact, we expect one. So why should a child not have a choice?

We had a variety of objects available, and we established that the children could have a choice, and they could work individually or in small groups to produce a short story based on their chosen object. We did not yet know the children or their capabilities, so it was important that no one should be restricted because of inability to produce written English. So the stories were spoken, and those who felt inadequate could be part of a group, and would have the feeling of belonging. As in many other sessions, we recorded the stories on tape.

Movement, as we knew it, was not familiar to the children, and they immediately reacted to a Russ Conway record with a rather agitated twist. At this stage we added to what was already there: "move only your legs," or "move only your arms," but over the weeks a vocabulary of movement was formed, using every part of the body as an instrument for movement. The standard of movement became extremely good, and was appreciated by the children, who would stand back and applaud an individual who had found a means of interpreting musical rhythm into physical body rhythm.

Music varied, sometimes popular music, at other times serious and complicated; but usually it was quite simple, and just as successful were simple sounds and silent pauses between beats from a tambourine. These children eventually reached a stage in the language of movement that was delightful to observe. It gave pleasure to others not taking part. We felt we had "arrived"— or had we? For on showing the children photographs of what they had been doing during previous weeks, they described what they could see in the photographs rather than what they had experienced.

We pursued this analysis over a period and, in co-operation with the class-teacher, would receive further written items carried out with photographs as reminders, in their own school. We found that these written comments, whether on movement or any other activity, followed a pattern, although there was the occasional exception.

(i) In photo number 9, Robert is there but I am not. There are a lot of other children with him, Susan and David and a lot more. Robert is dancing and David has his back to us.

(ii) The girl in the middle of the picture is Joanne, she is rather rude isn't she (Tongue showing). You can see Susan and Kim in the background, and you can see Jane and Margaret. I do not know what they are doing.

(iii) Peter is dancing to a record. I do not know the name of it, but I do know Peter fell over three times, and knocked against me once.

Sometimes we would find what might be the truth—

(iv) I am not in picture 10. Elaine, Margaret and Susan. We are all being floppy with Miss Arnott telling us what to do. Elaine is in the front. Margaret is in the middle and Susan is at the back. Miss Arnott has told us to be floppy dolls.

(v) This photograph shows Peter, he is near the blackboard, he is holding his chest. I think Miss Arnott has made a bang on the tambourine and we had to stand still.

But occasionally we would find the exception, as, for example—

(vi) My picture shows me moving, it looks as if I'm holding a baby. But I'm dancing and moving in my own way.

I don't care what anybody says. Miss Arnott was instructing us to do the movements we are doing: they are not real, they are make believe.

(vii) Picture no. 3 is of me doing a dance. I do not know what I was doing I just felt like it. I was in a sort of a dream at the time then there was a click he had taken a photograph of me in a funny position. I was wriggling and shaking.

We are not sure, at this stage, whether one can place any value on these comments, but one wonders whether we as adults (teachers) should assume that what we think must necessarily be the same as what the child thinks.

During the early days, "art" was linked with movement. Having translated a Russ Conway composition into terms of movement we would attempt to translate the music into terms of paint. Whether we can say honestly that anything positive was obtained from this activity is doubtful, although without exception every painting appeared related, and apparently sincere. This was made clear by such comments as: "You know the bit that goes like this, well, that's it there," or "That's when he stops playing for several seconds, and we have to freeze in our movement."

Apart from chairs, there were no tables for working upon, and all practical work was done on the floor. For the Russ Conway painting, a length of frieze paper would be stretched out the full length of the room, the children sitting on both sides, so that to the onlooker every alternate painting was upside down. The majority of children finished at about the same time and would announce this moment with "Finished." It was final, inviting no comment, and warning the teacher that there was no point in suggesting that one might try this or that. "Finished" really meant what it was intended to mean.

Some of the children would mark out their "territory" with a painted rectangle on the frieze paper before commencing, while others would make the same mark when their painting was finished. What we came to call "territory" often occurred in the two years we have been working together.

Because of the lack of furniture we had no pattern of seating, such as is found normally in most schools. When we got down to practical work on the floor, we observed that the majority of children worked in the same place continuously. A few worked in unusual places, under the blackboard, or in a corner out of sight of the main group. Some worked completely out of sight in the cloak-room area, while one small group worked close to the main door and often had to move because of the passage of people, but they always returned to their own spot. There were those who chose to work alone, while others preferred to work in a group so that friends could be together. There were one or two who preferred to move about continuously. This freedom to work wherever they desired created a happy working atmosphere.

This freedom of choice, to work where one wishes, does seem very important, and creates stability amongst most children (and adults). There is no doubt that to move children around in the classroom, or to re-arrange seating, or even to change completely the appearance of a room by removing all visual material, can in some instances lead to instability. If one must change, then the process should be gradual.

During the afternoon, fifteen minutes would be allowed for play. From the very beginning it was obvious that the play break was not being taken by all the children. Some continued to work; a small group would always be using the blackboard; others would be comparing work, and where the activity was different from their own, trying it out themselves. As the room often became hot because of the amount of glass used in the construction, and also because some windows had not opened since decoration last took place, children had often to be persuaded, sometimes with a little pressure, to take some fresh air, especially after an active period of movement. Despite this pressure, many children preferred to continue working. As the months went by, the number of children taking play lessened, and those who did go out were normally those children who had something planned for play. Eventually, when time for break was announced, the entire class responded with a definite "no," and echoed this reply weekly. Although the experienced teacher, over the years, would have had similar experiences with children over the break period, this was not lack of discipline or weakness on their part, but a protest at the unnecessary wastage of time.

In these days, an official period of play, or wandering about aimlessly in the playground, may be quite unnecessary, and this probably applies to infants who are learning through play. The school break is such a traditional right that it may be difficult to stop, and in its place to introduce a new form of voluntary break, when the need arises. Teachers do require a period of relaxation away from the classroom, at intervals, but it is doubtful whether children should have to take their period away from the classroom at the same time. It is interesting at this point to report that the Infant School which acted as our host on Friday afternoons has abandoned official playtime for children, who now wander quite sensibly out of the classroom, into the open, when the desire arises.

During the first term, movement and art were the weekly activities, and in both subjects the children were given a wide range of experiences, and in art the use of many materials and techniques. In many instances these were first experiences. The children came from a school which was very strong in English, and although we never deliberately attempted English as a subject, its influence was so strong that it quite naturally became as important an activity as movement and art.

Each week, as our Juniors arrived, they would have much to tell us about experiences they had had since our last meeting, and we would listen. At first it was quite casual, and we would stand attentively while they changed into clothing suitable for movement. Eventually, it became our first and main activity, and we would sit in a circle and talk together. Subjects would crop up quite naturally for discussion and debate, and, by the end of the year, discussion was taking up half the afternoon. Because this had come about quite naturally, both child and adult had found a natural level of understanding.

On many occasions we adults could withdraw completely from the debate, and listen to the subject under discussion thrown backwards and forwards, with true and natural use of vocabulary taking place. On occasions, those who came to watch our activities were a little bewildered and sometimes even a little unhappy at this sophisticated activity. But the regular observer could accept this; and indeed it did, if success can ever be achieved, become our most succesful activity.

We could now take almost any word, or subject, or a conversation, and pursue it, until we all felt enriched. For all contributors had something fresh to say, or an individual way of saying it, and words like memory, waterfall, dewdrop, texture, trees, relationship, environment, were pursued but never fully exhausted.

During these periods, when students were working with the children, it became possible to withdraw individuals and to have a conversation that time and circumstances would not normally permit in school. Children were invited to come and have a chat, but they were never persuaded or cajoled into coming. Some had very little to say, while others had much to talk about, and were pleased to find a listener.

We learnt quite a lot about a child's desires and anxieties, and, although we never intended to enter their private world, we discovered what underlay certain kinds of child behaviour. We are not thinking here of behavioural difficulties or disciplinary problems. We were a group of people working together, achieving together, living together, and so there was no problem of discipline. But behaviour in children is so varied that the opportunity to study and to talk to them as individuals made us realize how little we knew about them. Some needed our attention, and most wanted affection; one or two needed reassurance, and there were those who sought a father figure. One boy, each week, would have a poem, which he would recite, about things around him. It was very good poetry and taken quite seriously, but the father who was not living at home often appeared in the poems in various ways. A young girl whose only sister was in her twenties and was expecting her first baby, each week told us of all the excitement and of the preparation that was taking place at home. For several weeks the thoughts and joys of this child were shared with us, but just before the baby was expected, she was very worried that doctors might perform an operation on her sister in the same way that doctors can on animals, so that they could not have babies. After the baby was born, news would still flow in weekly, but one wonders whether we adults can cause conflict in the minds of children because of our inability to agree on a sensible form of sex education in school.

Through these individual conversations we became aware of the dreams of children and of their wishful thinking. One girl had very good reasons for wanting to be a bird, rather than a human, while others were more concerned with humanity and looking after the needs of those in distress. This desire took many forms, and even those who wanted to be actors wished to play the parts of doctors or nurses.

There were those who hoped that they might make adults happier than they appear to be at present. There was, for example, the girl whose mother believed that all her difficulties in life would disappear if only she had plenty of money. This girl accepted her mother's belief, and looked forward to making a lot of money and so bringing happiness to her mother.

Our activities with the children varied considerably, at times being carefully planned and at other times less rigorously so. Throughout we accepted as one of our criteria that the children should so enjoy themselves with us that they would not regret coming to us each Friday. As far as we could judge from the response of the children, from their remarks in casual conversation, and from the testimony of the class-teacher, we were successful in this attempt. Our work sometimes resembled that in their own school, and sometimes it differed since we had all the advantages of staffing, numbers and space. Sometimes the class-teacher was able to carry on our kind of work in the school.

In our efforts to learn about the children it was a great advantage to have the class-teacher with us because she was able to tell us quite a lot about the children and because she was qualified to correct some of our misconceptions. While she was able to point out those children who seemed to have gained most from the experience of coming to us, she reminded us that some of those, who were most active with us, were amongst the quietest in school, content to remain in the background. We had imagined that these were the bright or gifted Children, but they did not show up as such in class.

We felt and still feel that there is much to be said for schemes like ours for all children and that we have become much too accustomed to taking a static view of the school. Some children clearly benefit from a variety of environments, including new faces, new disciplines and relationships, and fresh approaches to education. We believe, as a result of our experiences in the last two years, with these children, that there should be more mobility amongst school-children so that some of those who are not entirely happy or who are not sufficiently inspired in their ordinary classroom (or in their schools, as for example in depressed areas) might for part of each week have a change of environment. Difficulties of transport are urged as insuperable barriers in the way, but surely at the present time the difficulty is not transport but cost of transport. Perhaps there is a still greater difficulty in our own static attitude of mind.

As has been intimated earlier, discussion developed into what was probably the most important part of the afternoon. To talk and talk, we felt, was the basis of what was to become worth while. It was to us as the sketch is to the artist. This was our common language, our natural way of communicating.

Our children were very young, but they were alive, were concerned with life, and were part of life. So they talked about most things within their living experiences, and occasionally we added other experiences to theirs.

We hoped that they would not see everything as black and white, but as a never-ending colour card of greys, that there was often no right or wrong answer, but a variety of possible solutions. We also hoped that through our relationships they would recognize that we were all individuals, and that we did not always think alike or see things alike. We could put a variety of interpretations on what we saw or heard, and this was one of the joys of being a human being, and why we had advanced intellectually as a species, although we had often done this without thought for other species of life.

We often listened to music, and we reacted as we naturally wished to do. We might just listen, or conduct, or play an imaginary instrument, but most often we found we had to move, often in an exciting and vigorous manner; and there were times when a melody became known immediately and was often asked for again. On one occasion we listened to the 1812 Overture, and afterwards painted our thoughts. We were not really concerned with the original story but rather with its effect on us. The results in paint varied, and yet there was something which all had in common; the composer might have been very satisfied. We listened also to recorded sounds, all concerned with ticking, and developing into the rhythm of machinery. Morse code suggested a variety of situations, and so did short details from a film sound-track.

We also looked at small details of ordinary things enlarged to a greatly increased scale, or many ordinary things repeated as a pattern. We found we could use these as inspiration for creative writing or painting. A small part of a leaf skeleton enlarged several hundred times would be seen as a paddy field, an aerial picture of a rural landscape, ice cracking, lightning, a hundred roads with a thousand paths, but it would eventually lead to vein structure, the nervous system, and finally to structure and construction itself.

At this point structure became the subject for discussion, and we looked for and discussed the mathematical and decorative structure of a rose window, leading to the Gothic cathedral, and then we compared medieval structures with modern design. This is the way things developed, and from an enlarged photograph of drain pipes seen as a piece of roadside sculpture by the photographer came the following poem—

Things from Outer Space

Steadily advancing
Laser guns blasting
Holes through ranks and ranks of tanks.

Tanks rumble forward,
Things that were,
Are no more.

They clash in combat,
Tanks move forward,
Things move back.

Then silence
The battle is won,
The things are no more.

This child may have been quite capable of writing a poem of this quality before meeting us, and he may not have required the photograph as a starting point. What is certain is that education cannot just be a series, or a knowledge of subjects which is finally tested. It is concerned with life, and in a minor way, along with many other people, we are part of the lives of these children and they have become part of ours. We think that we have all become enriched by having come together. We may even be more interesting, for it is doubtful whether anything of interest comes from an uninteresting person. That is why we talk so much about that which makes up life.

We had hoped that over a period of weeks we might pursue some topic and explore its possibilities, and the "Wild Wood" from *The Wind in the Willows* seemed to offer these possibilities.

We began once again with movement, and chose to work on spiky and smooth things. Our weekly discussions had reached that stage where talking would continue for some considerable time and where we would hardly have to intervene or re-direct if the discussion wandered off course. There was no limit to the vast range of things that were spiky or smooth and on one occasion we handled imaginary objects and observed a physical reaction to these, not only with the hands but with the face. In one discussion the children decided that spiky things could be placed into two groups, friendly and frightening respectively.

We painted these objects, and we also worked in clay. We modelled in clay spiky animals and smooth animals. Pieces of writing and short stories also evolved, based on these two starting points.

Monsters also emerged, usually friendly, and some that had yet to be discovered, although they existed at the time. Their appetites varied from those that lived under vast motor tyre dumps and throve on synthetic rubber, to those whose appetites throve on discarded dolls. In our dance, we covered a considerable number of movements using our limbs to express the qualities of spikiness and smoothness. We also found music which had these two qualities and we made musical instruments to which we moved, and which could also give those qualities.

Frightening, or to be frightened came under discussion, and we talked about frightening experiences we had had, and the effect they had on us at the time. In our movement we frightened others with the distorted movement of our bodies, and in turn suggested the experience of being frightened ourselves. We noticed that when children are excited in their play, they can express the sensation of being frightened extremely accurately, and we realized that they were genuinely quite frightened at what they were doing. This was gradually taken to a point where, together with the addition of voices, sounds and distorted faces and limbs, we formed a very frightening group of people. We again discussed what happened to us when we were frightened in real life, and its effect upon the body, as with tingling sensations, goose flesh, hair standing on end, inability to move, and that funny feeling in the stomach.

The chapter on the Wild Wood was read to the children by a student who was very capable of drawing the best out of its contents. The children did not give any indication that they were familiar with the story until the third week. As the story developed, they provided an atmosphere for it with background sounds—not overdone but as film music is used, there, yet not too obvious. We heard the wind whistling, the gentle patter of feet, and the creaking of branches.

It was during these periods of story-telling that we who were observing could study the children. For example, Susan always adopted a position close to the student for whom she had a deep affection, and we remembered that she had shown good dramatic qualities. Clare hung on to every word, her face revealing her inner feelings. Margaret, also following the story, caressed Kim's long hair; during tense periods in the story her hands would stop moving and would remain quite still, until the story levelled out again. This often happened in other ways and on other occasions, and we learnt to resist the temptation to draw attention to the activity, when we noticed a child doing three things at the same time. They were very capable of doing so.

We had a period of discussion in which we concentrated on trees only, looking at them out of doors, and talking about their life. Trees became personalities, and we looked closely at an individual tree nearby. We had also intended to wander through a nearby wood, but the inclement weather prevented this. We brought into the classroom several pieces of tree, bark and knobbly branches, rotted timbers and strange shapes. These pieces released considerable imaginative qualities from all the children.

It was important that there should be complete freedom of movement during this period, for there was considerable excitement as discoveries were made, and voices became very quiet as small groups discovered the possible causes of the unusual things that had happened to their piece of timber. It was equally important that the students could be approached easily, for a discovery had to be shared immediately, not only with their own age group but with the adult.

Later we had a look at the seasons and their effect upon trees, but we also chose one detail from the seasons, that of frost and its effect upon a tree, and found no difficulty in pursuing this for an hour. This may seem a long time for Juniors, but our children were capable of as much, and in any case they could bring the discussion to an end at any time they wished.

It is not always possible for many teachers to work "big," and the reasons are commonplace. But we were able to do so, and painted a very large mural of a wood. We had not thought of using this mural as a backcloth during its making, but it was actually used for this purpose by the children. Working "big" was quite a new experience for our children, for we had 1 inch and 2 inch brushes and vast quantities of paint, and so we worked on a large scale. These paintings of trees showed a wide range of development not only in painting but in observation. It would be more accurate to say that all the trees were different. In our movement we became trees, quivering, and leaning in the wind, and reaching up to the sky; we could be tall or short trees, or we might be old with short broken branches, or even become a mass of roots.

When given brush and paint, and the opportunity to choose that which interested them, most children painted the strange shapes and faces that appear among the trunks and branches of trees at dusk, while the remainder painted Mole. We were not looking for artistic pictures, but rather for what the children found amongst all the experiences of recent weeks. Then we left them alone to make, in their own way, a final comment on the Wild Wood. Their comment was a very simple one; they used their mural as a background, and gave the story in movement and drama, beautifully and sensitively produced, and containing only the essentials from what we had given them over the last few weeks.

But, despite all the planning and work that had gone into this, we had omitted the word "relief"—as experienced by Mole when Rat finally finds him in the Wood. The moment of relief, as portrayed by the two children playing the parts of Mole and Rat, suggested that they might not have needed us at all, and could very well have done everything alone.

We used clay on numerous occasions, and each time it was received with much enthusiasm. Despite their apparent enthusiasm, the children found it a very difficult material to manage, and their results were very disappointing not only to themselves but also when compared with work done by a similar age group which had already had experience in clay. We wondered whether children should discover for themselves the characteristics of clay or whether we should inform them. Should we teach technique so that ideas might be expressed in clay?

Our children showed considerable skill in the use of English language, but very little knowledge of the language of clay. They could write with facility, but with clay in the hand they showed limited manipulative skill. It does seem that clay (a means of expression) has arrived long after the other ways of expression which have already proved themselves.

Despite the many disappointments in the use of clay, enthusiasm for it remained high. The children tended to use it two-dimension-ally, and we tried to overcome this by insisting that we worked only seated in chairs. But in most cases the results were flat and still two-dimensional. It was a great temptation to teach and correct this, and eventually we had to do so, through the use of objects that were nice to feel.

Their attitude to this material was shown in their written work carried on in school—

Clay

Clay is a lovely thing
And you can make anything
    One can make a man or a castle
    A bowl or a parstle (sic)
    One can make a horse or a hen
    Or a funny thing like a pen.

Clay

Clay is very sticky it makes my hands all sticky and dirty. I have to smoothe the clay but it nearly always cracks again because it is dry. I never can finish the animal we sometimes have to make. Because I can never get my animals' legs out. But I think clay is fun to play with.

Clay

I think clay is nice and greasy and stogey. It feels funny if you push your fingers through it. You can push it, thump it and do what you like. It builds things and it can be broken.

To the observer we are a class, perhaps, with one or two students and a lecturer. But a great number of people are involved in this work, and most are unobtrusive. All have something in common—

not just a liking for children, or even for teaching, but a desire to understand children.

There is a feeling that we do not know very much about them, and now we know even less as a result of our study. Accepting this, we are all prepared to give up that nice safe way of teaching, and to be ready to find disappointment and lack of success. We want to try new things, though not necessarily to abandon the well-tried and proven ways.

We have to have a class, and a Head-teacher who has sufficient faith in us to hand the class over completely. We have to have a class-teacher who is willing to see all her principles and ways of working sabotaged, each Friday afternoon, and we have been fortunate in finding such a one. Our class-teacher is the main link between us and the children. We cannot do without her. She is there and she isn't. She is absolutely necessary and yet does not take part, but is aware of our activities and of what we are trying to do.

Our work is linked and used with the class work during the week. It is the class-teacher whose presence can maintain the stability that is so necessary for us, as our students vary considerably.

We have been welcomed into the Infant School each week, and have enjoyed its hospitality. We have felt wanted, and we know that there has been sympathy for our educational aims. We have brought the Infants in, to mix with our children. We have gone to see them at work, and they have come to see us.

We have all been part of a team, who were once strangers, but coming together with a common interest has brought to all of us, children and teachers, a feeling of satisfaction and a sense of being united in a worthy cause.

14 *Conclusion*

S. A. BRIDGES, M.A., B.Sc., Ph.D.

ALTHOUGH we do not feel justified in offering definite conclusions, we feel that the experimental work described has had its value. Apart from value in the Socratic sense that we now know how little we really know about the education of gifted children, the students and the staff of the College have benefited in a number of ways. Not only has the work been enjoyable for the children and ourselves but we have also been provided with useful material in our studies of children. We have also been brought into closer touch with the schools from which the children have come.

Our main results consist of a greater awareness in a number of fields, such as attitudes towards gifted children, the difficulties attending the approach to their problems, the needs of the children, the needs of the teachers of such children and the need for fresh approaches.

We have found a variety of attitudes to gifted children. Some of these have been based on fear that we were unduly favouring the children, others on political ideas of equality. Some teachers have shown themselves unhappy with gifted children, whose sense of humour is not always helpful in class. Some teachers do not know how to stimulate these children and mistake more complicated but often boring work for more challenging work. Levels of aspiration were often too low and children contented themselves with the performance expected by their teachers. The idea of a "stint" seems to develop early in schooling. More creative and open-ended work may gradually get rid of the "stint."

The gifted children revealed a variety of attitudes towards adults but generally settled down quickly to the relatively adult procedure and discipline of the College. Occasionally, when less experienced students took over, children temporarily reverted to more formal or more childish ways. Few of them showed any signs of the stereotype of the "Very Bright Child"; mostly they were just children, but they sometimes played down their abilities to be like the others.

Their basic needs are the same as for other children, e.g. affection, security and so on. In school they need understanding as others do: this understanding may be more difficult to achieve where the children are more gifted than their teachers. They also require adequate stimulation: it is not true that all they require is an opportunity for self-stimulation. This need is the greatest where the home does not provide it. This stimulation is not easy for the busy teacher with a large class: even in College, with plenty of help and expensive equipment, we were not always successful. Children of high ability can become bored easily, especially when they have to wait for slower workers. Repetition by teachers often irritates the gifted intensely. On the other hand we heard little complaint on the score of having to undertake undemanding work. As we have become aware of the variety of the causes of boredom we have modified our work in two ways, firstly by greater flexibility of the organization of group work and secondly by raising the standard of the challenge. Much of the challenge can come from their peers as well as from adults, and it does seem worth while to bring these gifted children together for part of each week. In these groups some of the activities should oblige the youngsters to co-operate, as in many cases their gifts tend to lead to some isolation from their co-evals. Conversation with intelligent and knowledgeable adults is of great value both intellectually and socially: such conversation is difficult in a classroom. Most of these youngsters have high verbal facility which sometimes misleads adults into thinking that they are more mature than they really are. Many of them show the need to be encouraged to think creatively or to try some divergent thinking.

Bibliography

1. Abraham, W. *Common Sense about Gifted Children*. New York, Harper Brothers, 1958.
2. A. S. E. *Science for Primary Schools*. London, John Murray, 1966.
3. Barron, F. *Creativity and Psychological Health*. Princeton, D. Van Nostrand, 1963.
4. Bassey, Michael. *School Science for Tomorrow's Citizens*. London, Pergamon Press, 1963.
5. Branch, M., & Cash, A. *Gifted Children*. London, Souvenir Press, 1966.
6. Brandwein, P. F. *The Gifted Student as a Future Scientist*. New York, Harcourt, Brace & World Inc., 1955.
7. Brigham, John E. *The Graphic Art of M. C. Escher*. London, Oldbourne Book Co., 1967.
8. Bruner, J. S. *The Process of Education*. Cambridge, Harvard University Press, 1962. *Studies in Cognitive Growth*. London, J. Wiley & Sons, 1966.
9. Burt, C. *The Gifted Child*. British Journal of Statistical Psychology, Vol. XIV, Pt. 2, 1961. *The Gifted Child*. Year Book of Education (Evans), 1962.
10. Burt, C., & Jackson, P. W. *Critical Notice: Creativity and Intelligence, by J. W. Getzels*. British Journal of Educational Psychology, 32, 1962.
11a. Cutts, N. E., & Moseley, N. *Bright Children, a Guide for Parents*. New York, Putnam & Co. Ltd., 1953.
11b. *Teaching the Bright and Gifted*. Englewood Cliffs, N. J., Prentice-Hall, 1957.
12. De Haan, R. F., & Havighurst, R. J. *Educating Gifted Children*. Chicago, University of Chicago Press, 1957.
13. Dunn, L. M. *Exceptional Children in the School*. New York, Holt, Rinehart & Winston Ltd., 1965.
14. Durr, W. K. *The Gifted Student*. New York, Oxford University Press, 1964.
15. Essex County Council. *Science and Mathematics for Primary Schools*.
16. Fitch Perkins, Lucy. *Cave Twins*. London, Jonathan Cape, 1922.

17. Fliegler, L. A. (Ed.). *Curriculum Planning for the Gifted.* Englewood Cliffs, N. J., Prentice-Hall, 1961.
18. French, J. L. *Educating the Gifted.* New York, Holt, Rinehart & Winston Ltd., 1959.
19. Gallagher, J. J. *Teaching the Gifted Child.* Boston, Allyn & Bacon Inc., 1964.
20. Getzels, J. W., & Jackson, B. W. *Creativity and Intelligence.* New York, J. Wiley & Sons, 1962.
21. Goldman, R. J. *The Minnesota Tests of Creativity.* Educational Research Vol. VII, No. 1, 1964.
22. Gordon, W. J. *Synectics.* New York, Harper & Row, 1961.
23. Gowan, J. C., & Demos, G. D. *The Education and Guidance of the Ablest.* Illinois, C. C. Thomas, 1964.
24a. Guilford, J. P. *Intellective Factors in Productive Thinking.* University of South California, 1963.
24b. Guilford, J. P. *The Structure of Intellect.* Psychological Bulletin, 53, 1956.
24c. Guilford, J. P. *Three Faces of Intellect.* American Psychologist, 14.8, 1959.
24d. Guilford, J. P. *Personality.* McGraw-Hill, 1959.
25. Henry, N. B. (Ed.). *Education for the Gifted.* University of Chicago Press (National Society for the Study of Education, 57th Year Book), 1958.
26. Hasan, Parween & Butcher. *Creativity and Intelligence.* British Journal of Psychology Vol. 57, Parts 1 & 2, 1967.
27. Hildreth, G. H. *Introduction to the Gifted.* McGraw-Hill, 1966.
28. Hollingworth, L. S. *Children Above 180 I.Q.* New York, World Book Company, 1942.
29. Hudson, L. *Contrary Imaginations.* London, Penguin, 1967.
30. Inhelder, B., & Piaget, J. *The Early Growth of Logic in the Child.* London, Routledge & Kegan Paul, 1964.
31. Jung, C. G. *The Development of Personality* (from Collected Works). London, Routledge & Kegan Paul, 1954.
32. Kogan, N., & Wallach, M. A. *Modes of Thinking in Young Children.* New York, Holt, Rinehart & Winston, 1965.
33. Langdon, Mrs. M. *Extended Course Work.* Brentwood College of Education, 1967.
34. Lovell, K., & Ogilvie, E. *The Growth of Concept of Volume in Junior School Children.* The Journal of Child Psychology and Psychiatry, Vol. 2, 1961.

35. Lowenfeld, Viktor, & Brittain, W. L. *Creative and Mental Growth.* London, Macmillan, 1966.
36. McKenzie, M. E. E. *The Major Achievements of Science.* London, Cambridge University Press, 1960.
37. Marsh, R. W. *Research Note on Getzels' & Jackson's Data.* British Journal of Educational Psychology, 34, 1964.
38. Mead, Margaret. Article in *Journal of Technical Education*, September, 1954.
39. Myers–Briggs, I. *Manual. Personality Indicator, Educational Testing Service.* Princeton, N. J., Prentice-Hall, 2nd Printing, 1962.
40. Osbourne, C. F. *Applied Imagination.* New York, Charles Scribner's Sons, 1957.
41. Parkyn, G. W. *Children of High Intelligence*, New Zealand Council for Educational Research, London, O.U.P., 1948.
42. Parnes, J., & Harding, H. F. *A Source Book for Creative Thinking.* New York, Charles Scribner's Sons, 1962.
43. Piaget, J. *The Origin of Intelligence in the Child.* London, Routledge & Kegan Paul, 1953.
44. Tannenbaum, A. J. *Adolescents' Attitudes towards Academic Brilliance.* Teachers College, Columbia University, 1965.
45. Taylor, C. W. *Creativity: Progress and Potential.* New York, McGraw-Hill, 1964. *Widening Horizons in Creativity.* New York, J. Wiley & Sons, 1964.
46. Taylor, C. W., & Barron, F. *Scientific Creativity.* New York, J. Wiley & Sons, 1964.
47. Taylor, C. W., & Williams, F. E. *Instructional Media and Creativity.* New York, J. Wiley & Sons, 1966.
48. Terman, L. M., et al. *Genetic Studies of Genius*, Stanford University Press, Vol. I, 1925; Vol. II, 1926; Vol. III, 1930; Vol. IV, 1947; Vol. V, 1959.
49a. Torrance, E. P. *Guiding Creative Talent.* Englewood Cliffs, N. J. Prentice-Hall, 1962.
49b. Torrance, E. P. *Education and the Creative Potential.* University of Minnesota Press, 1963.
49c. Torrance, E. P. *A Source Book for Creative Thinking.* Charles Scribner's Sons, 1962.
49d. Torrance, E. P. *Rewarding Creative Behaviour.* Englewood Cliffs, N. J., Prentice-Hall, 1965.
50. Unesco. *Source Book for Science Teaching.* London, Educational Productions Ltd., 1966.

51. Vernon, P. E. *Creativity and Intelligence.* Educational Research, Vol. VI, No. 3, 1964.

52. Waddington, M. *Problems of Educating Gifted Young Children with special reference to Britain.* Year Book of Education (Evans), 1961.

53a. Wall, W. D. *Highly Intelligent Children, Part 1. The Psychology of the Gifted.* Educational Research, Vol. II, No. 2, 1960.

53b. Wall, W. D. *Highly Intelligent Children, Part II. The Education of the Gifted.* Educational Research, Vol. II, No. 2, 1960.

Index